Natural Church Development

How your congregation can develop the eight essential qualities of a healthy church

Christian A. Schwarz

This international edition is published by
The Leadership Centre
British Columbia, Canada

Natural Church Development is available
in about 30 different language versions and in 50 countries.
All foreign language edition titles and addresses of distributors
can be found on the Internet:
www.NCD-international.org

Originally published as *Die natürliche Gemeindeentwicklung*
© 1996 Christian A. Schwarz
International rights: C & P Publishing, Diedersbüller Str. 6, D-25924 Emmelsbüll, Germany
Tel. ++49-4665-835, Fax ++49-4665-252, E-mail: institute@ncd-international.org

Canadian edition:
© 2002 The Leadership Centre
          P.O. Box 41083 RPO South
          Winfield, BC Canada V4V 1Z7
          Phone: 250-766-0907
          Fax: 250-766-0912
          Email: office@GrowingLeadership.com
          Website: www.GrowingLeadership.com

English-language Translation: Lynn McAdam, Lois Wollin, Martin Wollin
Cover Design: Heidenreich, Büro für Kommunikationsdesign
Printing: M.C.E. HOREB, Viladecavalls (Barcelona), Spain – Printed in Spain

Library of Congress Cataloging in Publication Data:
Schwarz, Christian A.
    Natural Church Development
    1. Church growth. 2. Evangelistic work I. Schwarz, Christian   II. Title
BV652.25.S34 1998   128 pages

ISBN: 0-9684097-0-9

04 03 02   5 4 3 2

Preface

Do you want to lead your church toward greater health? *Natural Church Development* will help you envision a more positive future. It will show you how to become more intentional in reaching your world with the message of hope and life in Jesus Christ.

Through *The Leadership Centre,* we are continually and prayerfully learning what God is about. Our goal is to collaborate with Him in what He seeks to bless. We see God raising up a new generation of pastoral leadership and developing new models of outward-focused churches.

Researcher Christian Schwarz and *Natural Church Development* are not only providing twenty-first century evaluation tools and technology so that churches can become islands of health. They also propose a significant paradigm shift through the "eight quality characteristics" of church health combined with the "minimum factor evaluation strategy." As Schwarz says, "There is one rule, however, for which *we did not find a single exception* among the 1000 churches surveyed. Every church in which a quality index of 65 or more was reached for each of the eight quality characteristics, is a growing church. *This is perhaps the most spectacular discovery of our survey.*" (emphasis added)

Christian Schwarz is not writing to debate various interpretations of the church growth movement. Rather, his passion is the Great Commission's focus on making disciples of all nations (see Matthew 28:19-20). His fundamental motivation is to "find a valid answer to the question, 'What should each church and every Christian do to obey the Great Commission in today's world?'" Realizing that many pastors are either discouraged or somewhat skeptical about their church's lack of turnaround, he seeks to dispel many myths and misconceptions.

Yet he also makes a very bold claim: "To my knowledge, our research provides the first worldwide scientifically verifiable answer to the question, 'What church growth principles are true, regardless of culture and theological persuasion?'" Can you afford to turn down such an offer? I believe he delivers on his promise. I urge you to prayerfully consider the truths underlying *Natural Church Development.*

G. John Baergen

"Natural Church Development *is not only providing twenty-first century evaluation tools and technology; it also proposes a significant paradigm shift."*

Natural Church Development

Away with technocratic thinking

"Saying good-bye to human success programs—and hello to God's growth automatisms."

Why is it that many Christians are so skeptical towards the church growth movement? Is it because they do not desire growth in their own congregations? Do they resent questioning the effectiveness of their church's ministry? Or is something other than the Great Commission their number one priority?

I don't doubt that there are people who fit these descriptions, but the criticism of currently accepted church growth principles does not come only from their circles. I have found many Christians with both a heart for the lost and a discerning method of ministry who for some reason have never embraced the church growth movement.

To them it seems to present simplistic rules and principles "that don't work in the real world, anyway." From their point of view, mere people are trying in their own strength to do what only God can do. Whether or not this impression is right, it is the image the church growth movement has in the eyes of many believers—a technocratic endeavor through and through, even in those cases where the spiritual aspect is emphasized.

Church growth in one's own strength

What does it mean to attempt church growth in one's own strength? Take a look at the cartoon below: a wagon with four square wheels, loaded with perfectly round wheels, pushed and pulled by two men. They are devoted, hard workers, but their job is slow, tedious, and frustrating.

For me this is more than a cartoon. It is a prophetic description of a large part of the body of Christ. The church is moving, but at a tediously slow pace. Why? If you asked the two workers, they would probably say, "It's because of the stiff resistance we encounter," or maybe, "We're going uphill, that's why!" And these answers are not all wrong!

As Christians we do encounter resistance at times, and a church's walk can be steeply uphill. The cartoon, however, helps us to understand that while such problems exist, the true cause

6

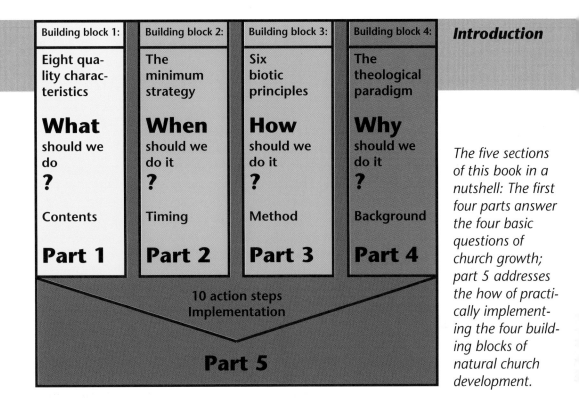

Building block 1:	Building block 2:	Building block 3:	Building block 4:
Eight qua-lity charac-teristics	The minimum strategy	Six biotic principles	The theological paradigm
What should we do **?**	**When** should we do it **?**	**How** should we do it **?**	**Why** should we do it **?**
Contents	Timing	Method	Background
Part 1	**Part 2**	**Part 3**	**Part 4**

10 action steps
Implementation

Part 5

The five sections of this book in a nutshell: The first four parts answer the four basic questions of church growth; part 5 addresses the how of practically implementing the four building blocks of natural church development.

for chronic frustration often has to do with something else—square wheels.

The illustration teaches us that God has provided everything we'll ever need for church growth, yet we do not always make proper use of it. That is the real problem. Instead of using God's means, we try to do things in our own strength—with much pulling and pushing.

That is what I mean by "technocratic church growth." It is not that the workers in this picture are unspiritual. It is not that their goal—to get the church moving—is in any way wrong. The problem is that their *methods* are insufficient because they are inconsistent with God's plan.

This book is based on a different approach to church growth. In my institute we have chosen to call it "natural," or "biotic" church development. "Biotic" implies nothing less than a rediscovery of the laws of life (in Greek, *bios*). The goal is to let God's growth automatisms flourish, instead of wasting energy on human-made programs.

The "biotic" alternative

What is natural church development?

> *"Some church growth concepts are so focused on the fruit that they fail to consider the root that produces that fruit."*

Why call our approach "natural church development?" Natural means learning from nature. Learning from nature means learning from God's creation. And learning from God's creation means learning from God the Creator.

To illustrate, I like to use the picture on the opposite page. It depicts several principles of organic growth. Most church growth authors would confirm the value of learning from these principles. The problem with many popular concepts, however, is that they fail to go deep enough. They are literally superficial: Thus they overlook the underground realities which influence life —like the composition of the soil, the workings of the root system, or the (very important!) role that worms play.

Why does the grass in this picture grow? Is it because of a numerical growth goal, such as "I will grow eight inches by the end of June 1997?" It could be that that is its secret (we will explore quantitative growth goals later). For now, I simply want to emphasize the need for recognizing the "underground" realities, without which we cannot answer the question of "why" there is growth. What happens below the surface is the strategic focus of natural church development.

Isn't this "natural theology?"

Applying observable laws and paradigms of nature to theology is highly controversial. I concede the difficulty here. This type of theological reasoning, called *theologia naturalis* can create enormous problems when applied to theology proper, i.e., the knowledge of God. It fosters the illusion that we can perceive and understand God on our own—without Christ, without the cross, without revelation. Here, however, we are dealing with *principles of church growth*, not with questions about the character of God. It seems to me that in this context, learning from creation is not only legitimate, it is a must!

Jesus Himself frequently used parables from nature and agriculture to illustrate the nature of the kingdom of God—the lilies of the field, the seed that grows by itself, the growth of the mustard seed, the four soils, the tree and its fruit, the laws of sowing and reaping. Some interpreters claim that Jesus used these examples simply because His audience lived in an agrarian society

8

Photo: Bayer, Leverkusen

The laws of organic growth: Some church growth concepts literally stay on the surface by merely studying the fruit, while overlooking the roots which produce the fruit

and therefore related best to such illustrations. I don't think that goes far enough. If Jesus were walking among us today, He would hardly replace these parables from nature with parables from the world of computers, such as "The kingdom of God is like a computer program—your output depends on your input." Technocratic illustrations like this would miss the secret of life. The sphere of the biotic has totally different laws from that of the abiotic.

Learning from the lilies of the field

A typical example of the biotic approach can be found in Matthew 6:28: "See the lilies of the field, how they grow." The word "see," however, does not fully cover the implications of the Greek word *katamathete*. This is the intensive form of *manthano*, meaning "learn," "observe," "study", or "research." Whenever in Greek *kata* is used in front of a verb, it usually intensifies the word. In our context it would mean to *diligently* learn, observe, study, or research.
What is it then that we are to diligently study? It's not the lilies' beauty, but rather their *growth mechanisms* ("how they grow"). We are to study them, examine them, meditate on them and take our direction from them—all these aspects are included in the imperative verb form *katamathete*. And we are told that we need to do these things in order to understand the principles of the kingdom of God.

Discovering the "biotic potential"

"The biotic potential is a concept designed by God the Creator Himself."

Every student of God's creation—Christians and non-Christians alike—will eventually stumble upon something scientists call the "biotic potential." Ecologists define it as the "inherent capacity of an organism or species to reproduce and survive." This is a concept entirely unknown in the world of technology. No machine is inherently able to reproduce itself. A coffee machine can make coffee (thank God!), but it will never make another coffee machine. In nature, however, the order of things is entirely different: a coffee plant produces coffee beans, which in turn can produce new coffee plants. It was God's intent to build this perpetuity into His creation from the start. It is the secret of life, a divine principle of creation.

When we are dealing with natural processes, it is important for this inherent potential to have free rein. The difference between the biotic potential and the empirical growth (in the laboratory as well as in the field) is called "environmental resistance." While it is clear that growth cannot be "made" or forced, it is important to keep the environmental resistance to a minimum in order to create the best possible conditions for growth.

The biotic potential in a congregation

The same is true for church development. We should not attempt to "manufacture" church growth, but rather to release the biotic potential which God has put into every church. It is our task to minimize the obstacles to growth (the "environmental resistance")—both inside and outside the church.

Since we have very little control over outside factors, we should concentrate on the removal of obstacles to church growth and multiplication within churches. Then church growth can happen "all by itself." God will do what he promised to do. He will grant growth (1 Corinthians 3:6).

The principle of self-organization

The principle of self-organization is found throughout creation. Secular system research uses the term "autopoiesis" (self-creating) for this phenomenon. It should rather be called "theopoiesis" (God-created). This principle brings a great mystery to light. If we apply it to the "organism church," we face the question of how to organize self-organization. What can be done to

Learning from God's creation: The principle of self-organization is evident every-where in nature, from the tiniest microorganisms to the laws governing the universe.

release the biotic potential—the growth automatisms, by which God Himself grows His church? The four building blocks of natural church development—quality characteristics, minimum strategy, biotic principles, new paradigm—try to supply an answer to this question.

Isn't that esoteric?

Much of the secular literature covering the topic of self-organization does have a significant esoteric bent which makes it more difficult to deal with this matter. The difference between the esoteric and natural church development, however, is much like the difference between astrology and astronomy!

Non-Christians who discover this phenomenon almost always tend to attach some pseudo-religious meaning to it. Instead of connecting self-organization with the only true God, the Father of our Lord Jesus Christ, the Creator of heaven and earth, a number of authors introduce fictional occult concepts. Although this does not change the divine origin of this principle— human misinterpretations of divine principles will never alter them—it nevertheless calls for a thorough biblical investigation and verification.

11

The "all-by-itself" principle

"The release of God's growth automatisms is the strategic secret of growing churches."

The term "growth automatisms" is at the heart of our definition of "natural church development" (see opposite page). The biblical concept behind this term is best described in the words of Mark 4:26-29: "And he was saying, 'The kingdom of God is like a man who casts seed upon the ground; and goes to bed at night and gets up by day, and the seed sprouts up and grows—how, he himself does not know. The earth produces crops *by itself*; first the blade, then the head, and then the mature grain in the head. But when the crop permits, he immediately puts in the sickle, because the harvest has come.'"

This parable clearly shows what people can and should do, and what they cannot do. They should sow and harvest, they may sleep and rise. What they cannot ever do is this: they cannot bring forth the fruit. In the text, we find the mysterious description of the earth producing fruit "by itself." Most commentators agree that this "by itself" is the key for understanding this parable. Just what does it mean?

The term used in the Greek is *automate*—literally translated it means "automatic." Thus this passage from Mark explicitly speaks of "growth automatisms!" Of course, to the Hebrew mind this automatism would never be credited to some god-like Mother Nature. In the context of the parable, the word means simply "with no apparent cause," and the underlying thought is "performed by God Himself." In applying this idea to the life of a congregation, it indicates that certain developments appear to happen "all by themselves," or "automatically." Christians, however, know—even though it cannot be proven empirically—that the fruit that develops seemingly *all by itself* is, in reality, a work of God. The "automatism" is really a "theomatism!"

The secret of growing churches

This is precisely what I mean by the "all-by-itself" principle. It is not merely a nice picture. I understand this principle to be the very essence of church growth. Growing churches utilize this principle. It is the "secret" of their success!

Some do it deliberately, others by instinct. It doesn't really matter. Ultimately, what counts is *applying* this principle. In fact, some even have faulty thinking about it. Their ministry may be *exemplary in practice* and a model from which to learn. But such churches' theo-

What does "natural church development" mean?

Releasing the growth automatisms, by which God Himself grows His church

Natural church development defined: All human endeavors are focused on releasing the divine growth automatisms.

ries are not able to accurately explain the secret of their growth, and they certainly cannot supply reproducible concepts for other churches. We will address this problem in more detail later.

I have discovered the principles of natural church development from three different sources:

The origin of natural church development

1. Through our **empirical research** of growing and non-growing churches. This does not mean, however, that we blindly accept the explanations churches give for their own growth or lack of growth.

2. By **observing nature**, that is God's creation. As we saw before, the Bible itself exhorts us to use this approach.

3. By **studying Scripture**. Throughout the Bible, we consistently encounter the biotic principles of church development—though not with these technical terms.

Neither the observation of churches nor of nature should ever become the basis for establishing absolute standards. If a concept contradicts biblical truth, Christians should reject it, even if it appears to have been used with "success." Not everything in nature is a "biotic principle" to be used in natural church development. Our task is to carefully and biblically discern what is theologically legitimate and what is not.

The major differences between natural church development and other church growth concepts can be expressed in three main points:

So what's the difference?

1. Natural church development rejects merely pragmatic and a-theological approaches ("the end justifies the means") and replaces them with a **principle-oriented** point of departure.

2. Natural church development has no quantitative approach ("How do we get more people to attend services?"), but looks at the **quality** of church life as the key to church development.

3. Natural church development does not attempt to "make" church growth, but to release the **growth automatisms**, with which God Himself builds the church.

Natural church development means bidding farewell to superficial pragmatism, to simplistic cause-and-effect logic, to a fixation with quantity, to manipulative marketing methods, and to questionable "can-do" attitudes. It means leaving behind human-made prescriptions for success and moving on to growth principles which are given by God Himself to all of His creation.

Three key terms In order to clarify the difference between natural church development and the predominant approaches, I will be using three terms throughout this book: the *"technocratic," "spiritualistic,"* and *"biotic" paradigms*. These terms are actually shorthand for entire outlooks on life which will be explained in more detail in Part 4 (pages 83-102). Once we understand the presuppositions on which these different patterns of thinking are founded, it is evident why natural church development cannot expect to find general acceptance among Christians.

Technocratic paradigm	**Spiritualistic paradigm**	**Biotic paradigm**
The significance of institutions, programs, methods, etc. is *overestimated*	The significance of institutions, programs, methods, etc. is *underestimated*	The theological approach underlying natural church development

Eight quality character- istics

Are there distinctive quality characteristics which are more developed in growing churches than in those which are not growing? And could it be that developing these quality characteristics is the "key to success" in growing churches, and beyond that, a more helpful approach than the pragmatic question, "How do we get more people to come to church?" This is precisely the focus of our research. The results put into question much of what until now has been marketed as "church growth principles."

Demythologizing church growth

"Learning from growing churches does not mean adopting the explanations church leaders often present as the key to success."

A look at church growth literature can be confusing. An entire array of programs claim, "Do what we do, and you will get the same results." Unfortunately many of these concepts contradict one another. One group pushes "megachurches" as the most effective way to reach a community with the gospel, while another suggests that the optimal church size is a small group, almost like most home Bible studies. Some suggest that the key to success is a worship service targeted toward non-Christians, while others emphasize that the goal of a worship service is exclusively worshipping God and equipping the saints. One group is convinced that marketing strategies must be integrated into church planning, while another enjoys healthy church growth without even having heard of such methods.

It appears to me that past discussions have made too little distinction between "models" (= concepts, with which some church in some part of the world has had a positive experience) and "principles" (= that which applies to every church everywhere). Thus some models parade as universally valid principles. At the same time, proven principles with universal application are sometimes mistaken for "one model among many."

Principles or models?

I have attempted to illustrate the difference between these two approaches in the diagram. When I talk about following a model, I mean a church's attempt to transfer the methods of a single successful church (most often a megachurch) to its own situation. This approach is especially fascinating because, to a certain extent, the vision one hopes to realize for one's own church is already visible in real life in the model church.

The *principle-oriented approach* is different. It also assumes that model churches have much to teach us. Yet rather than limiting itself to *one* extraordinary model, hundreds of model churches—both large and small—are researched to discover which elements turn out to be universal principles that are relevant for all churches—and which elements are perhaps interesting factors, but not generally valid principles for effective church growth. The principles are obtained by *abstraction*, i.e., by stripping the observable models of all their specific, local, and cultural flavor. In a second step, the principles thus gained are *individualized* for the concrete situation of a specific church. This

Models and principles

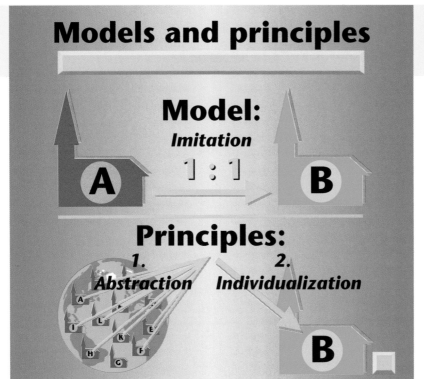

Model:
Imitation

1 : 1

A → B

Principles:
1. **2.**
Abstraction **Individualization**

B

While "imitation" best describes the process of simply copying the ministry of a single model church, the principle-oriented approach comprises two steps: "abstraction" and "individualization".

sometimes cumbersome principle-oriented approach (abstraction followed by individualization) is less attractive for some than the simple one-to-one imitation of a successful model church.

Natural church development, as described in this book, is a *principle-oriented approach*. There is nothing wrong with being inspired by a model church. However, if we want to go beyond enthusiasm to the transfer of reproducible elements, we must seek to discover the universal principles that are the basis for every kind of church growth.

Learning from growing churches means analyzing their practices to discover the universals. This means more than simply adopting the explanations church leaders often present as the key to success. I have learned each of the principles presented in this book from growing churches, and interestingly enough, often from churches that would reject "our" approach to church growth. It may well be that these churches would perceive their "success" in a completely different fashion, would use an entirely different jargon, and have never even heard of the principles of natural church development. Yet it can be demonstrated that they work and minister—consciously or unconsciously—according to these principles.

What does "learning from growing churches" mean?

The international research project

"This study developed into the most comprehensive research project of the causes of church growth ever undertaken."

How does one discover universally applicable church growth principles? Answering this question is not a matter of intuition, nor of studying a limited number of model churches. There really is only one way to find an answer to this question, namely, scientifically sound research of churches around the world.

This realization provided the framework for our research project. In order to accumulate a sufficiently large data base to make scientifically significant assertions, a minimum of 1000 different churches on all six continents was required. We needed large and small, growing and declining, persecuted and state-subsidized, charismatic and noncharismatic, prominent models and entirely unknown churches. We needed a cross-section of churches and regions where spiritual awakenings are occurring (such as Brazil or Korea), as well as areas which, in the light of worldwide standards, qualify more as "spiritually developing nations" (such as Germany).

This study developed into the most comprehensive research project of the causes of church growth ever undertaken. Churches from a total of 32 countries participated. The survey questionnaire, which was to be completed by 30 members from each participating church, was translated into 18 languages. In the end, we faced the task of analyzing 4.2 million responses. Those answers, cut out and pasted together, would create a band of paper extending from Chicago to Atlanta or from Los Angeles to Salt Lake City. To put it another way: if we were to take a walk along the equator and answer a question every ten yards, we'd be clear around the world before the last question was answered!

Why all the effort?

What motivated this massive endeavor was the realization that without such thorough research it would be impossible to decide which of the modern "principles of success" are universally applicable and which are simply "myths." Much of what is often matter-of-factly assumed to be a "principle of church growth" was shown by our research to be nothing more than the pet idea of a certain pastor. Such ideas, which are deduced from the personal experiences of one author, are not necessarily wrong. We can learn much from them. They are, however, not to be confused with universal church growth principles.

The research project

1000 churches, 32 countries, 6 continents

The research project conducted by Germany's Institute for Natural Church Development from 1994 through 1996 is the most thorough study to date of the causes for church growth. On the map, countries which participated in this study are colored red.

The scientific criteria

One of the most important criteria for our research project was a high scientific standard. Christoph Schalk, a social scientist and psychologist, agreed to coordinate the project and serve as its scientific advisor, after having identified several weaknesses in the testing procedures we had used until three years ago. He drafted a new questionnaire with rigorous standards for objectivity, reliability, and validity, and used approved methods from social science for the analysis of the data.

This project is actually the fifth stage in a series of research projects begun ten years ago in German-speaking Europe. Although the methodology may have left much to be desired in previous years, we gained an initial understanding of church growth principles upon which the subsequent studies were based.

The value of the research

To my knowledge, our research provides the first worldwide scientifically verifiable answer to the question, "What church growth principles are true, regardless of culture and theological persuasion?" We strove to find a valid answer to the question, "What should each church and every Christian do to obey the Great Commission in today's world?"

Is "growth" the appropriate criterion?

"Not every growing church is also a qualitatively 'good' church."

There is an unspoken assumption within the church growth movement that "growing congregations" are automatically "good churches." But is this equation accurate? We can find a great variety of statements on this subject in church growth literature, but in the end they are no more than opinions and hunches. The reason is simply that while *quantitative* growth in a church (size as well as growth rate) could be measured with a certain degree of accuracy, a reliable procedure for measuring *qualitative* growth with objective, demonstrable criteria was not yet available.

Our efforts over the past ten years have focused on developing this kind of evaluative instrument for churches. Having concluded our international research, we now have a procedure by which any church can determine its "quality index" (QI). This is based on the eight quality characteristics described on the following pages (For details see pages 38-39).

Four categories of churches

The picture at the top of the opposite page shows that in terms of the relationship between quality and quantity, four distinct categories of churches are identifiable.

a. *Quadrant top right:* churches with above-average quality (QI over 56, the mean of all above-average growing churches) and above-average quantitative growth in worship attendance (10 percent or more per year over a period of five years).

b. *Quadrant top left:* churches with above-average quality, but with diminishing worship attendance.

c. *Quadrant bottom left:* churches with below-average quality (QI less than 45, the mean of all declining churches) and diminishing worship attendance.

d. *Quadrant bottom right:* churches with below-average quality and above-average worship attendance.

With the insights gained from our research, we can finally quit speculating about these four types of churches. We have documented real life examples. The diagram bottom right shows the percentages of churches surveyed falling into each of the four categories. On the following pages, I will be using this basic dia-

Quality and quantity

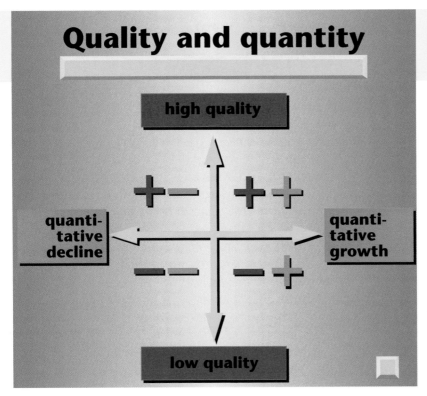

From the perspective of church quality and quantity, four different categories of churches are identifiable. Our research makes it possible to make significant conclusions regarding each of these four categories for the first time.

gram to illustrate the typical real life behavior of these churches in various areas.

When you encounter the "matrix of four" on the following pages, please do not assume that we surveyed only churches representative of these four categories in order to test the validity of our proposed principles. In order to determine which questions were the best indicators for the quality and growth potential of a church, we evaluated all of the churches that participated in the project, not only the 27% which fit into the categories on the diagram! However, the answers given by churches falling into these four specific categories in my opinion communicate most clearly the practical significance of the principles behind the questions.

The "matrix of four" as a diagram

Quality characteristic 1:
Empowering leadership

"The research data call into question the way most church growth literature uses megachurches to illustrate its leadership principles."

Church growth literature on the topic of leadership typically states that the leadership style of pastors in growing churches is more *project-* than *people-*oriented, more *goal-* than *relationship-*oriented, more *authoritarian-* than *team-*oriented. In their search for models worth imitating, some authors probably gravitate more towards *large* churches, which tend to employ this kind of leadership, than *growing* churches. The two, however, are far from being the same, as we shall see (pages 46-48).

Our research produced results different from what existing church growth literature (including my own writings) would have led us to expect. While it is correct that "goal-orientation" is an important leadership trait, it is interesting to observe that this is not an area where leaders of growing and non-growing churches differ greatly. Our study demonstrated that while pastors of growing churches are usually not "people-persons" who lose themselves in interaction with individuals, yet on the average they are somewhat *more* relationship-, person-, and partnership-oriented than their colleagues in declining churches (see graphic below).

The real difference The key distinction is probably best expressed by the word "empowerment." Leaders of growing churches concentrate on empowering other Christians for ministry. They do not use lay workers as "helpers" in attaining their own goals and fulfilling their own visions. Rather, they invert the pyramid of authority so that the leader assists Christians to attain the spiritual potential God has for them. These pastors equip, support, motivate, and mentor individuals, enabling them to become all that God wants them to be. If we take a closer look at this process, we understand why these leaders need to be both goal and relationship oriented. The "bipolarity" which will be explained as a theological paradigm of natural church development in Part 4, must be incarnated in the personality of the leader.

Leadership style

Are pastors of growing churches less relationship oriented?

	"Relationship oriented"	"Goal oriented"	"Partnership oriented"
Growing churches	45%	62%	70%
Declining churches	41%	63%	65%

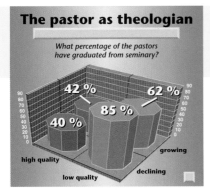

The pastor as theologian

What percentage of the pastors have graduated from seminary?

42 % 62 %
85 %
40 %

growing
high quality
declining
low quality

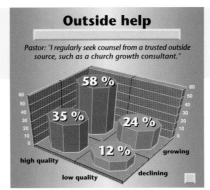

Outside help

Pastor: "I regularly seek counsel from a trusted outside source, such as a church growth consultant."

58 %
35 % 24 %
12 %

growing
high quality
declining
low quality

Two of the most interesting results regarding leadership: Formal theological training has a negative correlation to both church growth and overall quality of churches (left).

Among the fifteen variables related to leadership, the factor with the strongest correlation to the overall quality and growth of a church, is the readiness to accept help from the outside (right).

"Spiritual self-organization" in real life

What we encounter here was referred to in the introduction as the "all-by-itself" principle. Leaders who realize their own empowerment by empowering others experience how the "all-by-itself" principle contributes to growth. Rather than handling the bulk of church responsibilities on their own, they invest the majority of their time in discipleship, delegation, and multiplication. Thus, the energy they expend can be multiplied indefinitely. This is how spiritual "self-organization" occurs. God's energy, not human effort and pressure, is released to set the church in motion.

The research data call into question a tendency in church growth literature to illustrate leadership principles with examples from megachurches. In many instances, their materials showcase ingenious leaders who are so gifted that it is unrealistic to refer to their churches as "reproducible models." Now for the good news: pastors of growing churches do not need to be superstars. Most of the pastors with the highest scores in our survey are little known. They generally provide us, however, with more helpful basic leadership principles than most of the world-famous "spiritual superstars."

Why is there resistance?

It is obvious that the leadership model depicted here is popular with neither technocrats nor spiritualists. Technocrats tend to gravitate more towards a "guru," who can be either a classical cleric or a revered and aloof church growth manager. In contrast, spiritualists tend to have difficulty submitting to any form of leadership.

Quality characteristic 2: Gift-oriented ministry

The quality characteristic "gift-oriented ministry" demonstrates particularly well what we mean by "divine growth automatisms." The gift-oriented approach reflects the conviction that God sovereignly determines which Christians should best assume which ministries. The role of church leadership is to help its members to identify their gifts and to integrate them into appropriate ministries. When Christians serve in their area of giftedness, they generally function less in their own strength and more in the power of the Holy Spirit. Thus ordinary people can accomplish the extraordinary!

An interesting corollary result of our research was the discovery that probably no factor influences the contentedness of Christians more than whether they are utilizing their gifts or not. Our data demonstrated a highly significant relationship between "gift-orientation" ("My personal ministry involvements match my gifts") and "joy in living" ("I consider myself to be a happy, contented person").

None of the eight quality characteristics showed nearly as much influence on both personal and church life as "gift-oriented ministry." This is why it doesn't surprise me at all that the practical tools we have developed on this quality characteristic have had by far the best reception of all of our church growth materials. Here church growth is not merely a topic for a few church strategists; it is a crucial element for the life of each and every Christian.

Spiritual gifts and the "priesthood of all believers"

Unfortunately, in recent years some have misunderstood the gift-oriented approach as just another passing church growth fad. But the discovery and use of spiritual gifts is the only way to live out the Reformation watchword of the "priesthood of all believers."

How can this be achieved when Christians do not even recognize their God-given gifting and calling? According to a survey we conducted among 1600 active Christians in German-speaking Europe, 80 percent could not identify their gifts. This appears to me to be one of the primary reasons why the "priesthood of all believers" has, for the most part, never been achieved in the lands of the Reformation.

Resistance to the gift-oriented approach grows out of the false theological paradigms which persistently stifle and restrain much of Christianity. Technocratic thinkers tend to dictate which ministries lay-persons should assume and then search eagerly for "volunteers" to fulfill their vision. Should they not find any volunteers, they apply pressure. People must conform to their leader's preconceived framework.

In contrast, "spiritualists" often resist fitting their gifts into an established plan, since they are hostile towards church structures in general. From their point of view, it wouldn't be truly "spiritual." In addition, many of these spiritualists identify spiritual gifts exclusively with the extraordinary, spectacular, or supernatural, which of course keeps the gifts from being included in the church growth planning process.

Technocratic and spiritualistic resistance

Two of the ten questions with which we calculated the quality index for gift-oriented ministry: The question about the "use of gifts" (left) makes the difference particularly evident between above and below average churches. Of all the variables associated with this quality characteristic, the question on "lay training" (right) has the greatest correlation with church growth.

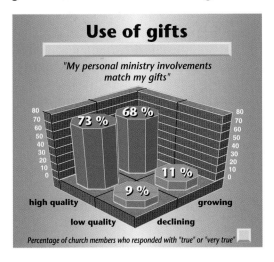

Use of gifts

"My personal ministry involvements match my gifts"

73 % 68 % 11 % 9 %

high quality   growing
low quality   declining

Percentage of church members who responded with "true" or "very true"

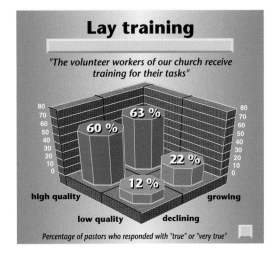

Lay training

"The volunteer workers of our church receive training for their tasks"

63 % 60 % 22 % 12 %

high quality   growing
low quality   declining

Percentage of pastors who responded with "true" or "very true"

Quality characteristic 3:
Passionate spirituality

"In churches which tend towards legalism, spiritual passion is usually below average."

Our research indicated clearly that church development is dependent neither on spiritual persuasions (such as charismatic or noncharismatic) nor on specific spiritual practices (such as liturgical prayers or "spiritual warfare" etc.) which are cited by some groups as the cause of church growth within their ranks. The point separating growing and non-growing churches, those which are qualitatively above or below average, is a different one, namely: "Are the Christians in this church 'on fire?' Do they live committed lives and practice their faith with joy and enthusiasm?" Since there are significant differences in this area between growing and declining churches (of various "spiritual cultures"), we called this quality characteristic "passionate spirituality."

The concept of spiritual passion and the widespread notion of the walk of faith as "performing one's duty" seem to be mutually exclusive. We noticed that in churches which tend towards "legalism" (where being a Christian means having the right doctrine, moral code, church membership, etc.), spiritual passion is usually below average.

Quality instead of quantity

The nature of this quality characteristic becomes evident by examining the prayer life of the Christians surveyed. While the amount of time (quantity) a Christian spends in prayer plays only a minor role with regard to the quality and growth of a church, whether prayer is viewed as an "inspiring experience" or not has a significant relationship to the quality and quantity of the church (diagram left). Similar results were found with respect to personal use of the Bible and other factors affecting personal spirituality.

This quality characteristic has been widely criticized in the past: "Passion alone is no reflection of one's loyalty to the truth." Even sects, so the argument goes, are characterized by great enthusiasm. This observation is true, of course. I have not yet

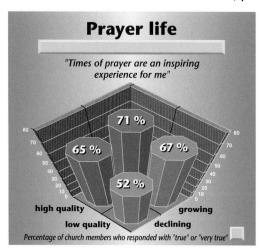

Prayer life

"Times of prayer are an inspiring experience for me"

71 %
65 %
67 %
52 %

high quality
low quality
growing
declining

Percentage of church members who responded with "true" or "very true"

Enthusiasm

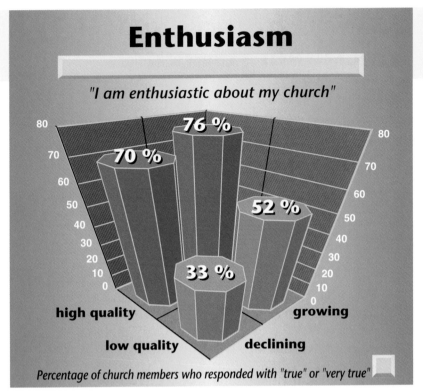

"I am enthusiastic about my church"

76 %

70 %

52 %

33 %

high quality

low quality

growing

declining

Percentage of church members who responded with "true" or "very true"

One of thirteen variables used in measuring the quality index for "passionate spirituality": Enthusiasm for the faith measured in churches with a high quality index nearly always correlates with enthusiasm for one's congregation.

researched the causes for growth among sects, but I suspect that their enthusiasm is likely a main reason for the impressive growth that some of these groups experience. This in no way validates the theological truth of their claims. Their doctrine remains theologically false, despite their enthusiasm and "successful" numerical growth.

On the other hand, "pure doctrine" alone, as countless examples illustrate, does not induce growth. A church, regardless of how orthodox its dogma and view of Scripture, can hardly expect to experience growth, as long as its members do not learn to live their faith with contagious enthusiasm and to share it with others.

Orthodoxy and passion

Wherever a "defense of orthodoxy" replaces the expression of a passionate faith in Christ, a false paradigm is at work. On such ideological ground, rigid fanaticism, but no truly liberated passion, will flourish. The quality characteristic "passionate spirituality" demonstrates empirically the theological core of the matter in church growth: the life of faith as a genuine *relationship* with Jesus Christ.

Quality characteristic 4:
Functional structures

"Wherever God breathes His Spirit into formless clay, both life and form spring forth."

Interestingly enough, "functional structures" proved to be by far the most controversial of the eight quality characteristics. The false paradigms which consciously or unconsciously influence most Christians are especially harmful in this area.

Spiritualists tend to be skeptical of structures, deeming them unspiritual, while those from the technocratic camp mistake certain structures for the very essence of the church of Jesus Christ. The traditionalists among them are more threatened by the adjective "functional" than by the noun "structures." "Functional" is to them an untheological, pragmatic, and unspiritual criterion.

Our research confirmed for the first time an extremely negative relationship between traditionalism and both growth and quality within the church (see diagram top right).

The real difference

The evaluation of the data from over 1000 churches on all continents was particularly interesting with regard to this quality characeristic. Despite the vast differences in structures from church to church within various denominations and cultures, those with a high quality index have certain basic elements in common. One of the 15 sub-principles comprising the quality characteristic "functional structures" is the "department head principle" (see diagram below left).

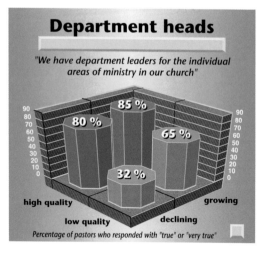

Department heads

"We have department leaders for the individual areas of ministry in our church"

85 %
80 %
65 %
32 %

high quality   growing

low quality   declining

Percentage of pastors who responded with "true" or "very true"

I have chosen this sub-principle because it typifies the core of this quality characteristic: the development of structures which promote an ongoing multiplication of the ministry. Leaders are not simply to lead, but also to develop other leaders.

Anyone who accepts this perspective will continually evaluate to what extent church structures improve the self-organization of the church. Elements not meeting this standard (such as discouraging leadership structures, inconvenient worship service times, demotivating financial concepts) will be changed or eliminated. Through this

Traditionalism

"I consider our church to be tradition-bound"

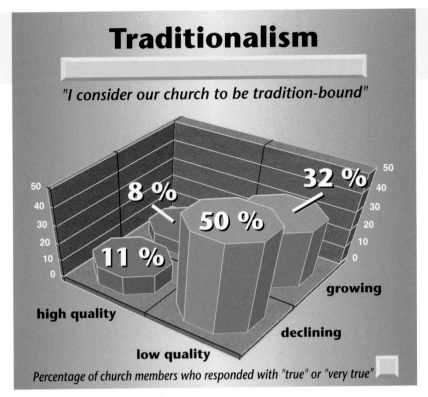

8 %

50 %

32 %

11 %

50 40 30 20 10 0

50 40 30 20 10 0

growing

high quality

declining

low quality

Percentage of church members who responded with "true" or "very true"

*Traditionalism as
a polar opposite
to the quality
characteristic
"functional
structures": While
only one in ten
qualitatively
above-average
churches struggles
with traditiona-
lism, every other
declining church
of lower quality is
plagued by this
problem.*

process of continual structural self-renewal, traditionalistic ruts can, to a large extent, be avoided.

One of the biggest barriers to recognizing the significance of structures for church development is the widespread view that "structure" and "life" are opposites. Interestingly enough, biological research reveals that dead matter and living organisms are not distinguished by their substance, as some people might think, but by the specific *structure* of the relationship of the individual parts to each other. In other words, in God's creation the living and nonliving, the biotic and abiotic are formed from identical material substances and are distinguished only by their structure.

This intimate connection between structure and life was first expressed at creation. The act of creation was an act of forming and shaping. The opposite of "form" is the unformed earth, the amorphous mass, the lump of clay. Wherever God breathes His Spirit into formless clay, both life and form spring forth. A comparative creative act occurs wherever God pours out His Spirit within the church today—and thus giving it structure and form.

Structures and life

Quality characteristic 5: Inspiring worship service

"There is probably no area of church life in which the important distinction between 'models' and 'principles' is so frequently ignored."

What is the common element that distinguishes the worship services of growing and declining, above- and below-average churches from one another? In other words, what should every church take into consideration in planning worship services? There is probably no area of church life in which the important distinction between "models" and "principles" (see pages 16-17) is so frequently ignored. Countless Christians believe that they must adopt certain worship models from other churches because they supposedly represent a particular church growth principle.

Our research shed some empirical light on the fog around the current discussion about worship services. Consider this example: many Christians are convinced that a church service which primarily targets the unchurched ("seeker service"), marvelously modeled by Willow Creek Community Church and others, is a church growth principle. I have spoken with numerous pastors who are in the process of changing their worship services into "seeker services," without ever having investigated whether this specific form of evangelism is appropriate for their context—for it is just one of many good approaches. They assume, however, that the "seeker service" is a universal principle. Yet it can be demonstrated that it is not.

The "seeker service" in the light of research

In our research, we selected all churches which reported a "very strong" orientation towards reaching non-Christians in their worship services. We found that this position was not typical of any single category of churches, neither growing nor declining, neither qualitatively above average nor qualitatively below average (see the left diagram on page 31).

This doesn't mean that the so-called "seeker services" are not a wonderful evangelistic method that a church might consider emulating. It simply means that this form of evangelism cannot be classified as a church growth principle. Services may target Christians or non-Christians, their style may be liturgical or free, their language may be "churchy" or "secular"—it makes no difference for church growth.

A different criterion proved to be the deciding factor, namely, "Is the worship service an 'inspiring experience' for the partici-

"Seeker service"

"Our worship service targets primarily non-Christians"

4 %   3 %   1 %   3 %

high quality   low quality   declining   growing

Percentage of church members who responded with "very true"

Inspiration

"Attending our worship services is an inspiring experience for me"

80 %   72 %   60 %   49 %

high quality   low quality   declining   growing

Percentage of church members who responded with "true" or "very true"

Part 1: 8 quality characteristics

While the question whether a church service targets primarily non-Christians (left) has no apparent relationship to church growth, there is indeed a strong correlation between an "inspiring worship experience" and a church's quality and quantity (right)

pants?" (see diagram above right). The answers to the eleven questions we asked churches about worship services all pointed in the same direction. It is this criterion which demonstrably separates growing churches from stagnant and declining ones.

The word "inspiring" deserves clarification. It is to be understood in the literal sense of *inspiratio* and means an inspiredness which comes from the Spirit of God. Whenever the Holy Spirit is truly at work (and His presence is not merely presumed), He will have a concrete effect upon the way a worship service is conducted including the entire atmosphere of a gathering. People attending truly "inspired" services typically indicate that "going to church is fun."

May worship services be "fun"?

Knowing this, the likely source of opposition to this quality characteristic becomes evident: Christians who go to church to fulfill their Christian duty. These people do not attend church because it is a joyous and inspiring experience, but to do the pastor or God a favor. Some even believe that their "faithfulness" in enduring such boring and unpleasant services will be blessed by God. Those who think this way will always tend to pressure other Christians to attend church. They have failed to comprehend the divine growth automatisms which are particularly evident in worship services. When worship is inspiring, it draws people to the services "all by itself."

The spiritualistic paradigm has a negative effect on worship services, too. Spiritualism suggests that "real spirituality" occurs exclusively in the "inner person." Such factors as a tasteful place of worship, a well-organized greeting team, a competent moderator, or a meaningful order of worship are unimportant for spiritualists or arouse the suspicion that they might contribute to the externalizing of the faith.

Quality characteristic 6:
Holistic small groups

"If we were to identify any one principle as the 'most important,' then without a doubt it would be the multiplication of small groups."

Our research in growing and declining churches all over the world has shown that continuous multiplication of small groups is a universal church growth principle. Furthermore, it has also disclosed what life in these small groups should be like if they are to have a positive effect on both quality and numerical growth within a church. They must be *holistic* groups which go beyond just discussing Bible passages to applying its message to daily life. In these groups, members are able to bring up those issues and questions that are immediate personal concerns.

Holistic small groups are the natural place for Christians to learn to serve others—both in and outside the group—with their spiritual gifts. The planned multiplication of small groups is made possible through the continual development of leaders as a by-product of the normal grouplife. The meaning of the term "discipleship" becomes practical in the context of holistic small groups: the transfer of life, not rote learning of abstract concepts.

Small groups or worship service?

One result of our research is highly provocative. We presented the following statement to the pastors we surveyed: "It is more important for us that someone be involved in a small group than attend church." We asked them to indicate the response that best described the situation in their church. The diagram at the bottom left illustrates that the same answer "no" was found in both growing and declining, in qualitatively above-average and below-average congregations. We can be sure that this is *not* a church growth principle, and therefore it does not determine the quality index of a church. It is a radical, fringe position.

And yet—if we take a closer look at the results we notice that this "radical, fringe" position is much more common in churches with above-average quality than in churches with below-average quality. This means that there is a greater tendency to give small groups priority over worship service attendance (in itself a

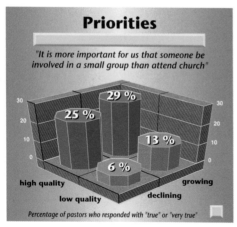

Priorities

"It is more important for us that someone be involved in a small group than attend church"

29 %
25 %
13 %
6 %

high quality   growing
low quality   declining

Percentage of pastors who responded with "true" or "very true"

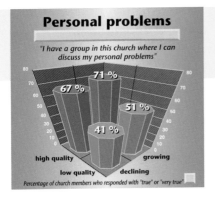

Personal problems

"I have a group in this church where I can discuss my personal problems"

71 %
67 %
51 %
41 %

high quality   growing
low quality   declining

Percentage of church members who responded with "true" or "very true"

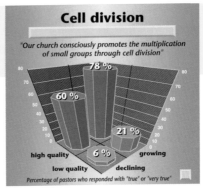

Cell division

"Our church consciously promotes the multiplication of small groups through cell division"

78 %
60 %
21 %
6 %

high quality   growing
low quality   declining

Percentage of pastors who responded with "true" or "very true"

Two of the twelve questions related to small groups whose answers reveal a strong relationship to the quality and numerical growth of a church.

strange alternative) in churches with a high quality index and in churches that are growing numerically. This still does not make the priority of small groups over worship services a church growth principle, for a principle is something that a church should not neglect under any circumstances. Nonetheless, it allows us to infer the level of importance given to small groups in growing churches: they are not a supplement, like a nice but dispensable hobby. No, much of the essence of true church life is worked out in small groups. Our research confirms that the larger a church becomes, the more decisive the small group principle will be with respect to her further growth.

After we had processed all 4.2 million survey answers, we calculated which of the 170 variables had the most significant relationship to church growth. It is probably no coincidence that our computer survey selected this variable in the area of "holistic small groups": "Our church consciously promotes the multiplication of small groups through cell division" (see diagram top right).

The "most important" question

If we were to identify any *one* principle as the "most important"—even though our research shows that the *interplay of all* basic elements is important—then without a doubt it would be the multiplication of small groups.

In order to give proper weight to the strategic importance of small groups, we have conceptualized nearly all of our church growth materials so that they can be used in small group contexts. We found that there is an enormous difference, for example, between church leadership discussing "evangelism," "loving relationships," or "gift-oriented ministry" in its staff meetings and having each Christian, integrated into a small group, go through a process in which he or she experiences the meaning of these terms practically expressed in the life of the group.

Small groups— the pillars of church growth

Quality characteristic 7: Need-oriented evangelism

"We must
distinguish
between Chris-
tians gifted for
evangelism and
those whom
God has other-
wise gifted."

Hardly any aspect of church growth is as riddled with clichés, dogmas, and myths as the area of "evangelism." This is true of those who view evangelism with skepticism as well as those who have made it their life calling. Most discussions about this topic have blurred the distinction between *methods* of evangelism that may have been used successfully by one or many churches and true *principles* of evangelism, which apply without exception to every church.

Unfortunately, "evangelism research" has limited itself to determining the effectiveness of individual evangelism *programs*. Without a doubt, this research can determine the "success" of such events, but it cannot show whether or not they represent universal *principles* (compare pages 16-17). Whenever a "successful program" is automatically presumed to be a "church growth principle"—a widespread Christian pastime—it causes tremendous confusion.

Every Christian an evangelist?

Our research disproves a thesis commonly held in evangelistically active groups: that "every Christian is an evangelist." There is a kernel of (empirically demonstrable) truth in this saying. It is indeed the responsibility of every Christian to use his or her own specific gifts in fulfilling the Great Commission. This does not, however, make him or her an evangelist. Evangelists are only those to whom God has given the corresponding spiritual gift. In one of our previous studies, we confirmed C. Peter Wagner's thesis that the gift of evangelism applies to no more than 10 percent of all Christians.

Who has the gift of evangelism?

We must distinguish between Christians gifted for evangelism and those whom God has otherwise called. If indeed "all Christians are evangelists," then there is no need to discover the 10 percent who really do possess this gift. In this way, the 10 percent with the gift of evangelism would be significantly under-challenged, while the demands on the 90 percent without the gift would be too great. This is a rather frustrating—and very technocratic—model. Our research shows that in churches with a high quality index, the leadership knows who has the gift of evangelism (see diagram right) and directs them to a corresponding area of ministry.

The gift of evangelism

Pastor: "I know which members of our church have the gift of evangelism"

70 %
65 %
43 %
21 %

high quality
growing
low quality
declining

Percentage of pastors who responded with "true" or "very true"

One of the most important principles of evangelism: Distinguishing between those Christians who have the gift of evangelism and those who do not have this gift.

It is the task of each Christian to use his or her gifts to serve non-Christians with whom one has a personal relationship, to see to it that they hear the gospel, and to encourage contact with the local church. The key to church growth is for the local congregation to focus its evangelistic efforts on the questions and needs of non-Christians. This "need-oriented" approach is different from "manipulative programs" where pressure on non-Christians must compensate for the lack of need-orientation.

What every Christian should do

It is particularly interesting to note that Christians in both growing and declining churches have exactly the same number of contacts with non-Christians (an average of 8.5 contacts). Challenging Christians to build *new* friendships with non-Christians is most certainly not a growth principle. The point is rather to use *already existing* relationships as contacts for evangelism. In each of the churches we surveyed—including those that lamented having little or no contact with "the world"—the number of contacts outside the church was already large enough so that there was no need to emphasize developing new relationships with the unchurched.

Making use of existing contacts

35

Quality characteristic 8: Loving relationships

"Growing churches possess on the average a measurably higher 'love quotient' than stagnant or declining ones."

Some years ago, when we published materials to help individuals, groups, and entire churches learn how to express Christian love, some specialists said that these were not "church growth materials." Yet our research indicates that there is a highly significant relationship between the ability of a church to demonstrate love and its long-term growth potential. Growing churches possess on the average a measurably higher "love quotient" than stagnant or declining ones.

To determine this "love quotient," we asked (among other things) how much time members spend with one another outside of official church-sponsored events. For example, how often do they invite one another over for meals or a cup of coffee? How generous is the church in doling out compliments? To what extent is the pastor aware of the personal problems of the lay workers in the congregation? How much laughter is there in the church? Two of the twelve variables which comprise the "love quotient" are pictured in the diagrams to the right.

We found that these issues, which some strategists discounted as irrelevant, contain important church growth principles. To put it even more pointedly, whereas a "seeker service" cannot be called a church growth principle any more than an "evangelistic crusade" or the practice of "spiritual warfare" (as valuable as they may be), it can be demonstrated that there is a significant connection between "laughter in the church" and that church's qualitative and numerical growth. It is interesting that such a significant factor, which according to the data definitely has the status of a church growth principle, receives almost no mention in church growth literature.

The results of Christian love

Unfeigned, practical love has a divinely generated magnetic power far more effective than evangelistic programs which depend almost entirely on verbal communication. People do not want to hear us talk about love, they want to experience how Christian love really works. The more technocratic a church, the more difficulties it will have in living out the Christian commandment to love. Since the technocratic paradigm understands faith primarily as the fulfillment of dogmatic and moral standards, it produces a deficit among Christians in their ability to love.

Laughter

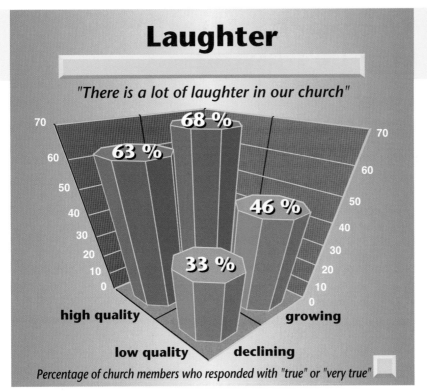

"There is a lot of laughter in our church"

68 %

63 %

46 %

33 %

high quality

growing

low quality   declining

Percentage of church members who responded with "true" or "very true"

The question of whether there is much laughter in a church has a strong correlation to the quality of a church and its growth. Interestingly enough, aspects like this find little mention in church growth literature.

The romantic notion of love

The spiritualistic paradigm is just as detrimental in its effect on a church's love potential. In contrast to the biblical definition of love—as fruit, action, or deed—these churches espouse a rather secular concept of love. Love is viewed as a *feeling* which overwhelms you (if you're lucky) and then disappears just as mysteriously. According to this perspective, it is impossible to empirically measure the love potential of a church, and all planned efforts to increase this potential are considered useless from the start.

It is interesting to note that the most frequent "minimum factor" of churches with more than 1000 in attendance is the quality characteristic "loving relationships." But wherever there is a lack of love, further church development is severely hampered.

Hospitality

"How often have you invited someone from the church over for a meal or a cup of coffee in the past two months?"

17 x

16 x

13 x

11 x

high quality   growing

low quality   declining

Average calculated for one year

No quality characteristic may be missing

"No church wanting to grow qualitatively and quantitatively can afford to overlook any one of these eight quality characteristics."

The real challenge of our international research project was to develop an empirical method for measuring the eight quality characteristics (which had already proved to be relevant to church growth in our pre-studies), and for comparing them to one another. We developed numerous questions corresponding to each of the eight areas, which, among other things, were to fulfill the following two criteria:

a. They had to show an empirically demonstrable connection (factor and item analysis) to the other questions on the same scale (= the same quality characteristic).

b. They had to show a demonstrably positive connection to the quantitative growth of the church (criteria validity).

In each of the countries we surveyed, the values we obtained were normed to a median of 50, i.e., the "average church" for each country had a quality index of 50 for each of the eight characteristics. The result of the study was that growing churches clearly scored above the qualitative median in each of the eight categories, and declining churches were similarly below the median (see diagram right).

It all depends on the interplay

Our research tells us that there is no one single factor which leads to growth in churches; it is the interplay of all eight elements. No church wanting to grow qualitatively and quantitatively can afford to overlook any one of these quality characteristics. For example, the widespread claim that "church growth is exclusively a matter of prayer" is simply not true. Such a statement absolutizes one element of the quality characteristic "passionate spirituality" at the expense of all the others. If this claim were true, it would mean that church development is possible without cultivating love, without making use of spiritual gifts, and without evangelism. This viewpoint is not only empirically untenable, it is also contrary to Scripture—a false teaching. Much prayer but little love, few gifts, and no evangelism? That would be strange indeed! Examples like this demonstrate once again the inherent contradictions of the "spiritualistic paradigm."

Neither small groups nor worship services, neither leadership nor structures, nor any other element is "the" key to church

Survey results

Growing and declining churches vary significantly in all eight quality areas

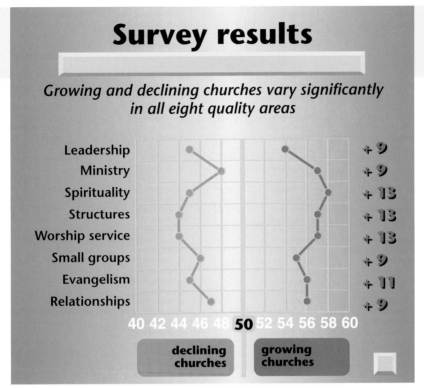

Leadership	+ 9
Ministry	+ 9
Spirituality	+ 13
Structures	+ 13
Worship service	+ 13
Small groups	+ 9
Evangelism	+ 11
Relationships	+ 9

40 42 44 46 48 **50** 52 54 56 58 60

declining churches   growing churches

There is a qualitative difference between growing and declining churches: The survey of over 1000 churches on all six continents indicates that on the average, growing churches have a higher quality index in all eight areas than declining ones.

growth. "The" key is found in the harmonious interplay of all eight elements. We should be wary of advice to follow someone's pet emphasis that excludes the other quality characteristics.

Based on the data we compiled, we were for the first time able to empirically prove the following three theses:

Three significant conclusions

1. The differences between growing and declining churches in all eight quality areas are highly significant. Thus, growing churches have—on the average—measurably higher quality.

2. There are, however, exceptions to this rule: churches which grow numerically, but have a below-average quality index. Quantitative growth is apparently attainable by methods other than the development of the eight quality factors (such as effective marketing, contextual factors, etc.).

3. There is *one* rule, however, for which we did not find a single exception among the 1000 churches surveyed. Every church in which a quality index of 65 or more was reached for each of the eight quality characteristics, is a growing church. *This is perhaps the most spectacular discovery of our survey.*

The "65 hypothesis"

> **"This is one of the few church growth principles for which we have yet to find a single exception anywhere in the world."**

The proposition that there is a qualitative value beyond which quantitative growth will *always* occur (in exact statistical terms: a probability of 99.4 percent) may sound preposterous at first. Yet the data do not allow for any other interpretation. Upon closer investigation, however, this phenomenon no longer appears so surprising. Just what does it mean for a church to have reached a quality index of 65 in all eight areas?

If we deliver such a statement from the abstraction of statistical language, it means the following: this is a church in which the leadership is committed heart and soul to church growth; in which nearly every Christian is using his or her gifts to edify the church; in which most members are living out the faith with power and contagious enthusiasm; in which church structures are evaluated on whether they serve the growth of the church or not; in which worship services are a high point of the week for the majority of the congregation; in which the loving and healing power of Christian fellowship can be experienced in small groups; in which nearly all Christians, according to their gifts, help to fulfill the Great Commission; in which the love of Christ permeates almost all church activities. Is it even conceivable that such a church could stagnate or decline?

Whenever I visit churches where the "65 hypothesis" holds true, I always have a strong pervading sense of the presence of the Holy Spirit. What others find "objectionable" with this hypothesis is not the churches which prove its accuracy. No, what is objectionable—or, perhaps more accurately, unfamiliar—is the process which attempts to express deeply spiritual axioms in empirical categories.

Less than 65 may also do

The "65 hypothesis" most definitively does not maintain that every church that wants to grow must have attained a quality index of 65 in all eight areas. This qualitative value is actually quite high. The vast majority of growing churches have noticeably lower values. The "65 hypothesis" simply states that whenever all eight values climb to 65, the statistical probability that the church is growing is 99.4 percent. Again, this is one of the few church growth principles for which we have yet to find a single exception anywhere in the world.

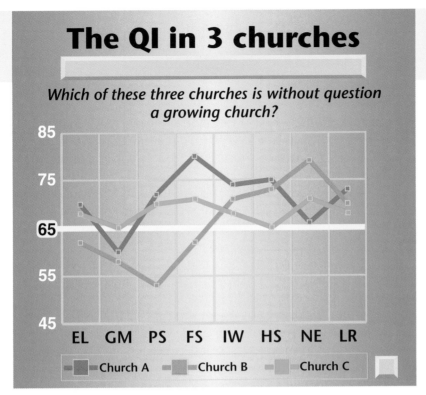

The QI in 3 churches

Which of these three churches is without question a growing church?

85

75

65

55

45

EL GM PS FS IW HS NE LR

Church A   Church B   Church C

The quality indices of three different churches: According to the "65 hypothesis," church C is doubtless a growing church (EL = empowering leadership; GM = gift-oriented ministry; PS = passionate spirituality; etc.).

Please note the above diagram. It shows the profiles of three of the churches we surveyed. According to this diagram, church A has the highest measurable quality and church B the lowest. Can we determine simply by looking at this graph which of these three churches is growing numerically? Based upon the "65 hypothesis" it is possible to say that church C is—with 99.4 percent certainty—a growing church, since all eight quality index values are at 65 or above.

When asked what must happen to attract more people to our worship services, I can only offer one scientifically defendable reply: "We must work at reaching an index of 65 in all eight quality areas." My answer may not be very popular, but it is true. Why then does it so seldom enter into discussions about increasing attendance?

No easy road

Just so that I am not misunderstood, the "65 hypothesis" by no means presumes that it is easy to achieve this kind of growth. Moreover, this is not some gimmick or quick fix method that promises push-button instant growth. It is—this is the hard reality—a difficult path.

The qualitative approach

"In natural church development our point of departure is not outward manifestations of growth, but the qualitative causes."

The qualitative approach, as described in the previous sections, has tremendous significance for practical ministry. Our fundamental question is not "How do we attract more people to our worship service," but rather "How can we grow in each of the eight quality areas?" Behind this question is the solid conviction—both theologically and empirically founded—that genuine quality will ultimately positively impact quantitative growth.

In natural church development, our point of departure is not outward manifestations of growth, such as increased worship attendance, but the spiritual and strategic causes behind them, as described by the eight quality characteristics. The "65 hypothesis" referred to earlier appears to me to be proof that the "all-by-itself" principle described in the introduction is more than a nice theory. It can be demonstrated that this principle really works. This shouldn't surprise us, since it is God-given. What we describe with imperfect words is nothing but a human effort to gain a better grasp of a divine principle.

Quality produces quantity

On the basis of these empirically demonstrated facts, I am decidedly against the widespread church growth movement thesis which states that developing quantity requires a *different* set of methods than developing quality. We now have every reason to come to the opposite conclusion. Precisely the same "methods" which produce higher quality will generate quantitative growth as a natural "by-product."

In the light of our survey, it seems very questionable to repeatedly take "growing churches" (a purely quantitative criterion) as a standard. On the previous pages we have seen enough examples of "growing churches" of below average quality. These are churches in which most Christians do not recognize their gifts, where little love is practiced, where passionate prayer seldom occurs, where there is little enjoyment of one another, and not much to laugh about. Yet they are growing. If "growth" indeed were the sole issue here, then we should turn to these churches to discover their "recipe for success." Yet there is hardly anything to learn from them! I would even venture to say that we

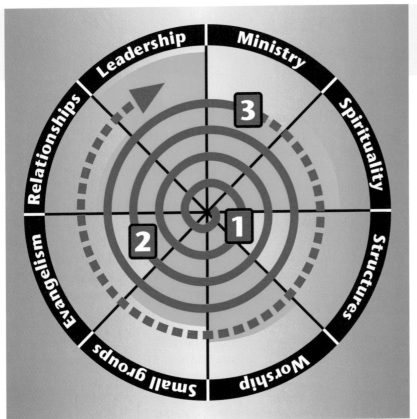

*The relationship
between qualita-
tive (blue area)
and quantitative
growth (red spi-
ral) in a church:
According to
natural church de-
velopment, qual-
ity determines the
development of
worship service
attendance. The
weakest quality
characteristic
("minimum fac-
tor") plays the
critical role.*

can learn much more from declining churches with above-average quality (a rare phenomenon) than from growing churches
with below-average quality. If this sounds preposterous, I would
recommend a quick review of the diagrams presented on pages
22 through 37 contrasting these two categories. This should convince even the strongest proponents of the quantitative approach that the orientation towards church quality is by far the
more helpful point of departure.

Some church growth specialists react very negatively to the
qualitative approach because it has been misused in the past.
Until now, it was all but impossible to accurately measure the
quality of church life. This allowed churches that have never experienced numerical growth to self-righteously refer to their supposedly high quality—which they presented as being far more
important than numbers. This is no longer possible. Our research
shows that the lack of quantitative growth in most cases indicates
a qualitative problem. Above a certain qualitative level, there are
no stagnant or declining churches at all.

**Opposition to
the qualitative
approach**

Why quantitative growth goals are inadequate

"Seven out of ten fast-growing churches do without quantitative goals—and apparently fare exceedingly well."

In many church growth books we meet a stubborn myth: a church that wants to grow needs numerical growth goals such as, "By the year 2002 our worship attendance will have reached 3,400." If there is any one challenge that most of the Christian public identifies with the church growth movement, this is it. Yet our study revealed that only 31 percent of all above-average growing churches use such goals. In other words, seven out of ten fast-growing churches do without them—and apparently fare exceedingly well (see diagram). This statistic alone does not say much about the usefulness (or harm) of quantitative growth goals, but it does point out that we are not dealing with an universal church growth principle.

The meaning of goals

So as not to be misunderstood, let me emphasize that I know of no growing church that can do without the motivating power of concrete goals. Churches need precise, challenging, time-bound, and measurable goals in order to progress in their development. But expressing such goals in terms of worship service attendance appears to me to be rather shallow. Just how should a statement such as "In the near future 3,400 worshippers will gather in our sanctuary" serve as a concrete source of motivation? Of course, one can marvel at the numbers, but it still does not motivate individuals to take concrete steps towards church growth.

I think something basic has been overlooked here. Goals can only motivate people when they touch on areas which they can personally influence. The magic number of 3,400 is in and of itself hardly motivating—and a fixation on such figures can actually be counterproductive. For how can one little church member make any meaningful contribution?

However, to become more loving towards other home group members; to cordially welcome guests at our worship services; to invite unchurched acquaintances over for

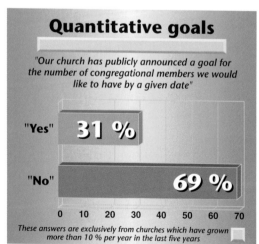

Quantitative goals

"Our church has publicly announced a goal for the number of congregational members we would like to have by a given date"

"Yes" **31 %**

"No" **69 %**

0   10   20   30   40   50   60   70

These answers are exclusively from churches which have grown more than 10 % per year in the last five years

coffee; to commit oneself to pray at a certain time each day—these are all attainable goals which members can personally influence. And isn't it interesting that a concentration on these qualitative areas *demonstrably* has a stronger relationship to a church's growth than the supposedly important attendance goals?

The distinction between what is "humanly possible" in a church (e.g., improving the quality of ministry) and what is not (e.g., increased attendance, conversions)—we will discuss this in more detail in Part 4—has practical implications. We must make sure to set goals only in areas of human "achievability," and not in areas that are beyond our control. Could it be that some church growth authors advocate worship attendance numbers as "goals" because they quietly assume that this is actually humanly possible? As we have observed, this illusion is characteristic of the technocratic paradigm.

The difference between goals and results

Of course it is not wrong, but rather very useful to track worship attendance and to analyze trends—it all depends upon the value assigned to attendance statistics. Increased worship attendance is not the ultimate "goal," with everything else being a means to that end; it is a natural by-product of improved quality.

This insight leads to an important conclusion. Because increased church attendance is the natural effect of higher quality, it follows that monitoring attendance can serve as a strategic instrument for "success control." This instrument, along with other indices, helps us to find out whether our work on the quality of church life has borne fruit. As we have seen, increased worship attendance alone does not prove the quality of a church. Nevertheless, if a church experiences no quantitative growth whatsoever over the years, then it has every reason to seek the causes in clearly identifiable qualitative problems.

Qualitative rather than quantitative goals

The point of departure for natural church development is, therefore, not goal setting in the area of quantity ("3,400 in church by 2002"), but in the area of quality ("By the end of November, 80 percent of all regular worship attenders will know their spiritual gifts"). In *this* area, we dare not neglect setting challenging, attainable, time-bound, and measurable goals.

Are large churches "good" churches?

"On nearly all relevant quality factors, larger churches compare disfavorably with smaller ones."

Those familiar with church growth literature regularly encounter the names of a number of large churches which are held up as models to be imitated. The presupposition is that *large* churches are by definition *good* churches. Is this thesis tenable? Our research revealed for the first time that the opposite is probably true. I would like to describe step-by-step how we came to this conclusion during the course of our research project.

1. We sensed that there was something in it when we analyzed the data and compared the average membership and worship attendance figures of growing and declining churches (see the first of the two diagrams on the left): declining churches averaged twice as many members as growing churches, and their worship attendance was on the whole 17 percent higher.

2. In another step, we checked on real growth rates in both "large" and "small" churches over the past five years (bottom left diagram). The average in smaller churches was 13 percent, whereas in larger churches it was a mere 3 percent. A statistically significant difference was also evident on the quality index. Large churches typically scored two points below the median of 50, small churches two points above the median.

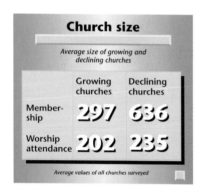

Church size

Average size of growing and declining churches

	Growing churches	Declining churches
Member-ship	297	636
Worship attendance	202	235

Average values of all churches surveyed

3. We then calculated which of the 170 variables that served as the basis for our survey had the strongest *negative* correlation to church growth. The astonishing result: church size turned out to be the third strongest negative factor, on a par with factors like "liberal theology" and "traditionalism!"

Quality and growth

Relationship between the size of churches and their quality and quantity

	Large churches	Small churches
Annual growth rate	3%	13%
Quality index (QI)	48	52

"Small" = under 100 in worship five years ago
"Large" = over 300 in worship five years ago

4. In order to define "large" and "small" more precisely, we examined sets of churches of specific sizes: those with 1-100 worshippers, 100-200, 200-300, 300-400, and so forth (see diagram top right). The result? The growth rate of churches decreased with increasing size. This fact in and of itself came as no great surprise, because in large churches the percentages represent many more people. But when we

Growth performance

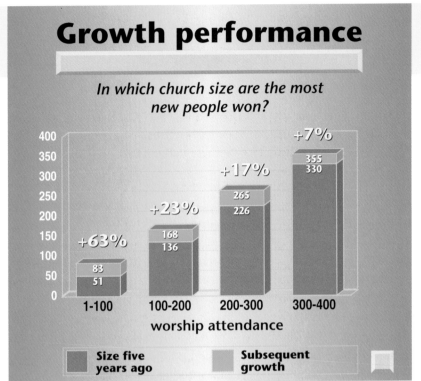

In which church size are the most new people won?

400
350
300
250
200
150
100
50
0

+63% 83/51
+23% 168/136
+17% 265/226
+7% 355/330

1-100   100-200   200-300   300-400

worship attendance

■ Size five years ago   ■ Subsequent growth

With increased church size, the growth rate rapidly decreases, while the number of new individuals won to a church remains relatively constant at about 30 persons in all four size categories (over a five-year period).

converted the percentages into raw numbers, we were dumbfounded. Churches in the smallest size category had won an average of 32 new people over the past five years; churches with 100-200 in worship also won 32; churches between 200 and 300 averaged 39 new individuals; churches between 300 and 400 won 25. So a "small" church wins just as many people for Christ as a "large" one, and what's more, two churches with 200 in worship on Sunday will win twice as many new people as one church with 400 in attendance.

5. But couldn't it be that the picture is different for *really* large churches (with more than 1000 at worship services)? Our huge reservoir of data enabled us to test this theory for the first time. Here are the results: While the smallest churches (with an average attendance of 51) typically won 32 new people in the last five years, the megachurches (with an average attendance of 2,856) won 112 new persons during the same time period. In raw numbers, a single megachurch won many more people than a single "minichurch" (see diagram page 48, top left). If we remember, though, that the megachurches are 56 times the size of the "minichurches," then the following calculation expresses the potential of the two categories

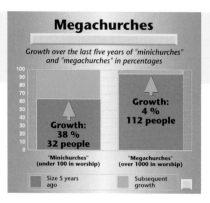

Megachurches

Growth over the last five years of "minichurches" and "megachurches" in percentages

Growth:
38 %
32 people

Growth:
4 %
112 people

"Minichurches"
(under 100 in worship)

"Megachurches"
(over 1000 in worship)

Size 5 years ago

Subsequent growth

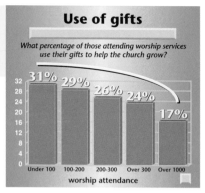

Use of gifts

What percentage of those attending worship services use their gifts to help the church grow?

31% 29% 26% 24% 17%

Under 100   100-200   200-300   Over 300   Over 1000

worship attendance

Left: "Megachurches" and "minichurches" compared. Right: An example of diminishing quality with increasing church size.

far more realistically. If instead of a single church with 2,856 in worship we had 56 churches, each with 51 worshippers, these churches would, statistically, win 1,792 new people within five years—16 times the number the megachurch would win. Thus we can conclude that the evangelistic effectiveness of minichurches is statistically 1,600 percent greater than that of megachurches!

6. On nearly all relevant quality factors, larger churches compare disfavorably with smaller ones. Here are just two examples. In minichurches (under 100), 31 percent of all in attendance have, according to the pastor, an assignment corresponding to their gifts; in megachurches, this figure is a mere 17 percent (diagram top right). In minichurches, 46 percent of those who attend services have been integrated into a small group, whereas in megachurches this is true of only 12 percent. The scenario is just as dramatic for nearly all of the 170 variables which we used to rate a church's quality.

Rules and exceptions to the rule

Aren't there any examples which might demonstrate just the opposite—churches which are large and at the same time growing numerically and characterized by high quality? Yes, there are such churches. And they are so unique, so exceptional that they are the talk of the whole world ("news is what is different"). They are truly the exception to the rule, indeed quite spectacular exceptions.

We should rejoice that these examples exist. Yet we should avoid making these churches into models for others. It seems to me to be far more helpful to carefully examine the countless smaller churches manifesting high quality, strong growth, and innovative multiplication. If we need models at all, we should look for them in this category.

The minimum factor

Christians who have learned the principles of natural church development may protest, "And am I supposed to think of all of this at once? I can't see the forest for the trees." This is the time to apply what we call the "minimum strategy." To begin with, it is sufficient to concentrate on one single area. Which area is strategically the most decisive? Our research confirms once again that an agricultural analogy, concentration on the so-called "minimum factor," plays a significant role. The minimum strategy is the biotic answer to the question of good timing in church development.

Focusing
our energies

"The minimum strategy helps a church to do less than before—but more of the right things."

Example of a church profile: The minimum factor is the quality characteristic "holistic small groups."

The minimum strategy assumes that the growth of a church is blocked by the quality characteristics that are least developed. If a church focuses its energy primarily on these minimum factors, this alone can lead to further growth (see the graphics below and right).

Natural church development is not a matter of always doing more. Actually, it should help us to do less than before—but more of the right things. Our limited resources should be concentrated on the spiritually strategic key factors. The story of David and Goliath illustrates what this kind of concentration of energy can accomplish. Goliath was unquestionably the stronger of the two, but David fought with God-given intelligence. First, he concentrated his strength with the help of his sling, by which he was able to multiply the effect of the energy released. Second, he struck precisely the most effective point, namely Goliath's forehead.

In a similar way, a hornet can disable even an elephant if it uses its "power" effectively. While in technocratic thinking small causes have only small effects, within an integrated system even very small causes can have enduring effects.

In Part 1 (pages 40-41) we explained that when all quality characteristics in a church reach a quality index of 65 (or more), there is a nearly 100 percent certainty that this church is a growing one. This "65 hypothesis" already indicates the strategic importance of the minimum factor. As soon as a church reached the 65 index, quantitative growth resulted in all the churches we surveyed, without exception.

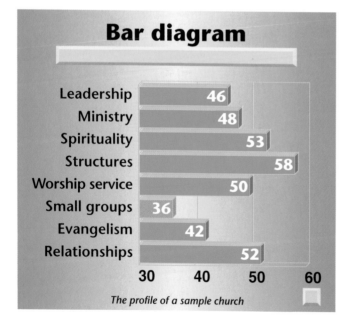

Bar diagram

Leadership	46
Ministry	48
Spirituality	53
Structures	58
Worship service	50
Small groups	36
Evangelism	42
Relationships	52

30   40   50   60

The profile of a sample church

As we analyzed the data of all 1000 churches from different viewpoints, it became clear that raising a church's quality index can be best achieved by improving the minimum factor.

Of course, the minimum strategy does not rate the minimum factor higher than other factors. As we have seen, natural church development calls for the harmonious interaction of all eight quality characteristics. This means that, in one sense, a church should work on all eight factors simultaneously.

The minimum strategy is simply a tool to help us set timely priorities. Since we can't work on all eight areas with the same amount of energy and concentration we need to find areas which will yield the greatest long-range return on our investments.

Obviously, the minimum factor will differ from church to church. While "functional structures" may be the quality characteristic that proves to be the deciding point in church A, "passionate spirituality" is the critical factor in church B and "empowering leadership" in church C. Each church must discover its own key area, and refrain from imposing its own experience and conclusions on others!

The profile of the same church is here presented in "helix" form (helix = spiral, see pages 96-97). The blue areas show how strongly developed the individual quality characteristics are. The red spiral reflects the development of the worship attendance. In this case, further growth is inhibited by inadequate small groups.

Even within a single church, different characteristics can be the minimum factor at different times. The minimum factor can change relatively quickly, particularly when there is a conscious attempt to improve on this one area.

Every church profile (including the one illustrated in the two diagrams of these pages) reflects only one moment in time, and may be quickly outdated.

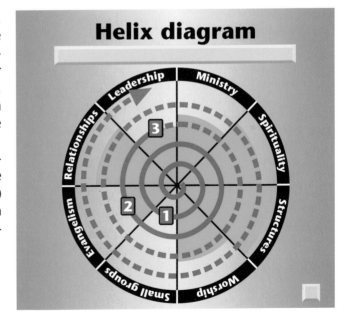

Helix diagram

The minimum barrel

"The shortest stave determines how much water the barrel can hold."

It has been my experience that most Christians are more easily convinced by a simple demonstration than by a discriminating scientific analysis of the principles of natural church development.

I have had a "minimum barrel" built to use in my seminars (like the one to the right). It is nothing more than a tub with staves of varying lengths. When I visit a church for which a church profile has been prepared, I write the names of the eight quality characteristics on the staves according to how strongly or weakly each of the individual characteristics is developed. The name of the minimum factor (e.g., "structures") is written on the shortest stave and the name of the maximum factor (e.g., "spirituality") on the longest.

The spiritual significance of the minimum factor

Then I pour water into the tub until it starts to overflow. While I am pouring and the carpeting or the feet of those sitting in the front row are getting wet, I ask the participants what I should do.

Some, including the custodian, demand that I stop pouring the water immediately. I don't, of course, because in this illustration the water symbolizes God's blessing flowing down from heaven into the church. We can't seriously want to ask God to stop blessing us just because our church has trouble "holding the water!"

Others suggest that we should pray more. I agree that prayer is extremely important and absolutely essential for church growth. Then I extend the longest stave, "passionate spirituality," four inches—and everyone can see that this noble measure doesn't solve the real problem. The water keeps splashing down onto the floor.

Eventually someone suggests that I should lengthen the minimum factor stave. And look at that! As soon as I lengthen it just one inch, the tub can hold more water!

Why do I mention this example? Because the dynamics behind the minimum strategy (both statistical and spiritual) are relatively complex. We will never be able to motivate others for this ministry approach without the help of convincing illustrations.

The minimum barrel

*The shortest stave determines the amount of water
the barrel can hold*

"Service
attendance"

"Minimum
factor"

"Quality
characteristics"

*In this picture of
the minimum bar-
rel, the staves
represent church
quality and the
water, the quan-
tity. This clearly
illustrates the sig-
nificance of the
minimum factor
for church devel-
opment.*

**God's work and
human work**

Such analogies demonstrate well the central issues in church development. The barrel comprised of eight staves (= quality characteristics) represents what we can and, according to God's will,
should build. Admittedly, our industrious improvements in the
quality of the tub cannot cause the water (= newly won people)
to flow into it. If God does not send water, even the finest barrel
will stay dry.

On the other hand, if and when God pours out the water—and
there is much theological evidence for the fact that He does so
most willingly—then the quality of our "barrel" (= church) is decisive. This quality ultimately determines whether the barrel can
hold any water at all.

**The limits of
illustrations**

Of course, just as with biblical parables, we must not confuse the
literal and figurative meanings of such illustrations. At some
point, every analogy breaks down. However, as long as we remember not to stretch the point, these object lessons are very
useful tools for teaching the basics of natural church development: the relationship between God's work and humankind's,
between quality and quantity, between improving all eight factors at the same time and the minimum factor in particular.

Parallels from agriculture

As with all the building blocks of natural church development, the minimum strategy is inspired by examples from biology. It is based on discoveries about the use of fertilizers made some 150 years ago by Justus von Liebig, a biologist and chemist.

Liebig discovered that four minerals are necessary for the growth of a plant: nitrogen, lime, phosphoric acid, and potash. As long as all four minerals are present in the soil in sufficient amounts, growth occurs automatically. Development stops, however, when one of the minerals is depleted (diagram 1). Should this deficiency be overcome, i.e., the missing nutrient applied, the plant will continue to grow until another of the minerals is depleted (diagram 2). If phosphoric acid were then used again to prompt further growth, because it had worked so well in the past, then the deficiency could now become an excess (diagram 3). The surplus of phosphoric acid actually poisons the soil. The more the farmer tries to correct the condition by applying phosphoric acid, the more his yield shrinks and the greater the damage to the environment. If a different fertilizer is applied, however, eliminating the deficiency in another area (diagram 4), growth will again be stimulated.

The minimum-oriented fertilization overcame the supposed "natural law of decreasing yields," and a sudden increase in agricultural productivity resulted—while the farmers who followed this strategy didn't need to invest in any additional resources!

Why "experience" is not transferable

Transferring these principles to church life makes it astoundingly simple to explain a frequently observed phenomenon. One pastor (farmer) works hard and does almost exactly what he sees his neighboring pastor doing. However, his efforts yield no fruit while the neighboring church experiences explosive growth. Month after month, the second pastor tries to convince his colleague to emphasize evangelism just like he does. The first pastor follows this well-meant advice but things get even worse.

The "successful pastor" is like a farmer who has doubled his harvest by fertilizing with phosphoric acid, and thus recommends phosphoric acid as the cure-all to every problem. What he doesn't realize is that the solution to his problem may actually be counterproductive in someone else's situation!

54

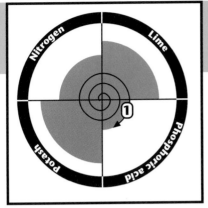

Diagram 1: While three of the four vital nutrients (potash, nitrogen, lime) are available in adequate amounts, plant development is hindered by insufficient phosphoric acid.

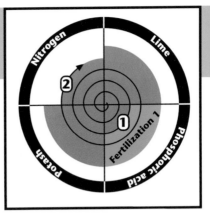

Diagram 2: After phosphoric acid is added, growth continues until development is slowed by insufficient nitrogen.

Diagram 3: Should the farmer follow his past experience and fertilize with phosphoric acid (a procedure which proved effective in the past), the fertilization will either have no effect or prove harmful, since an excess of phosphoric acid can make the soil overly acidic. Plant growth is limited in this case by insufficient nitrogen.

Diagram 4: If fertilizer is applied specifically to the new minimum factor, there are two effects. First, growth continues; second, the soil, which was acidified by excess phosphoric acid, is automatically decontaminated.

Minimum or maximum factor?

"The minimum strategy does not teach us to concentrate on our least capable areas."

Over the past years, the minimum strategy has been so convincing for some Christians, that they have begun to apply it as a general behavioral model for all areas of life. Thus, in some churches the watchword became, "We should always concentrate on the area in which we are the least capable." Obviously, with this kind of philosophy, frustration is preprogrammed!

The minimum strategy does not teach us to concentrate on our least capable areas. This misunderstanding comes from isolating the principles demonstrated by the "minimum barrel" from the whole of natural church development. In some areas of church life, we must work from our strengths (the area of spiritual gifts is one example) and in other areas (for example, the "fruit of the Spirit" as described in Galatians 5:22) our primary focus should be on our weak points. The question of whether we should concentrate on strengths or weaknesses proves to be a false alternative.

Why building on our strong points doesn't always help

What does this mean for the church as a whole? As long as nonessential ministry elements are at issue, we should develop our strengths and not pay undue attention to weaknesses. For example, if one of the strong points of a church is its liturgical, artistic worship, including organ music, then it should develop this strength and use it in other areas. This church could target culturally-oriented people and invite them to worship services, rather than trying to introduce hand clapping and tambourines to complement the organ music. The same thing could be said of all nonessential elements of church life (neither organ music nor tambourines are essential to church development).

However, when we are dealing with the *vital signs* of a church—the eight quality characteristics are in this category—we can no longer ignore shortcomings. As long as even just one of the quality characteristics is missing or underdeveloped—for example, "functional structures"—developing the strengths in another area, such as "passionate spirituality," will not help, since growth is not blocked by deficient spirituality, but by nonfunctional structures. We must restore the organism to good health before seeking further growth in our areas of strength.

Strengths and weaknesses

Using strengths to work on weak areas

Leadership	58
Ministry	68
Spirituality	63
Structures	55
Worship service	50
Small groups	48
Evangelism	44
Relationships	63

20 30 40 50 60 70 80

If the greatest strength of a church is, for example, "gift-oriented ministry," and the minimum factor is "need-oriented evangelism," then it should use the identified gifts to further the ministry of evangelism.

We have found that it is best to combine both approaches, i.e., using the current strengths of the church to work on the weakest point. If the greatest strength is "gift-oriented ministry" and the greatest weakness "need-oriented evangelism," as in the diagram above, it would be wrong to declare that "our spiritual gifts are no longer important; from now on we will focus only on evangelism." That would be a highly unproductive strategy indeed!

It would be much better to say, "From now on, let us better use the wonderful gifts God has given each one of us to fulfill the Great Commission." This is the kind of approach that characterizes the strategy of natural church development as a whole. We don't press a church into a predetermined program. Instead, we take what God has already given to the church and ask, "How can we better use this for His glory and the growth of His church?"

Use strengths to work on the minimum factor!

Beware of "models"!

We have just seen the ambiguous effects of trying to superim-pose one church's success story upon another. Just as phosphoric acid is not the answer to all agricultural problems—as important as this mineral may be to plant growth—no single individual quality characteristics is the solution to all church problems.

Neither "empowering leadership," "gift-oriented ministry," "passionate spirituality" nor any other quality characteristic is the key to church growth. And should a church find that improving one particular quality characteristic proves to be the key—and some do experience this—then it is highly probable that they have intuitively identified their minimum factor. There is absolutely no indication that an emphasis on this area would bring about the same results in another church.

"Experiences" prove nothing

I emphasize this point because so much of what is written on church growth today offers no better advice for churches than the slogan "phosphoric acid is the answer for all farming problems all over the world." Pastors for whom one of the eight quality characteristics has become particularly important often start selling it as the solution to the problems of other churches. But when a portion is promoted as the whole, it smacks of ideology. If our research proved anything, it was this: a reduction of church growth to a few areas of ministry is untenable.

Thus caution is advisable whenever one bases their theses on their own experiences alone. While personal experiences provide terrific testimonies, they do not necessarily *prove* anything.

The difference between illustrations and proofs

Are personal testimonies then of any use at all? Though experiences do not *prove* anything in themselves, they often beautifully *illustrate* what has been proven. Such illustrations have a greater, more convincing psychological effect on most people than scientific evidence. A vivid, convincing object lesson for many people effectively constitutes almost a "proof."

In my own ministry, I try to do justice to these educational principles. I do all I can to make sure that the principles I present are proven to be universally applicable. When communicating an idea to others, however—in a seminar, for example—I refer only

	Description	**Goal**	**Incorrect use**	**Correct use**
Testi-mony	Description of personal experience, which often emphasizes the opposite of what normally happens	People should be enthused by the power of God	"I must experience what this person or church has experienced"	"What a great experience that church had! Let's see what God has in store for us"
Model	A church's experiences are presented in such a way that reproducible structures can be identified	People should be motivated by a real-life example to do something similar themselves	"If I want to achieve the same success, I must imitate the model church exactly"	"I may well imitate a model church for a while in order to discover the universal principles which also apply to me"
Prin-ciple	The essence distilled from hundreds of models; the most important criterion is universal applicability	Churches should know and apply the laws of growth which are fundamental for every form of church development	"These principles are just one of many possibilities for building the church of Christ"	"I try to apply these principles to my individual situation"
Pro-gram	Application of (ideally) universal principles to one or more actual situations	Churches are to be helped with practical steps, using positive experiences of others as a kind of pattern	"If a program has worked for me, it will certainly be right for other churches, too"	"I choose a program based on universal principles which fits our situation—or I develop one on my own"

sparingly to research results and use anecdotes, stories, pictures, and personal experiences instead.

The minimum barrel demonstration which I described (see page 52) *proves* absolutely nothing, except perhaps that each barrel can only hold a certain amount of water. Nevertheless, it is a powerful tool to *illustrate* something which has already been painstakingly proven. We should *never* confuse psychologically convincing analogies or anecdotes with validated statements. Confusing the two causes the jumbled chaos of personal testimo-

The differences between testimonies, models, principles, and programs. Each has value, but they should not be confused with one another

nies, models, principles, and programs (see chart on the previous page) which persistently characterizes typical church growth discussions.

"Do it the way we do!" The confusion of "personal experiences" with "universal principles" happens especially with regard to successful churches which are—rightfully—honored as "model churches." Much of what these churches assert about church growth is outstanding. Other things, however, touted as universal principles, cannot be proven to be such. Yet observers often consider the size of the church to be of itself adequate "proof" that the tenets are true and therefore applicable to other churches.

When someone starts talking about their personal experiences, portraying them as universal principles, alarms should go off. "What worked for me will work for you" is a red flag statement!

The importance of model churches I do not mean to suggest that we should not learn from model churches. Hardly anything unfreezes ingrained church routine better than seeing a vital, dynamic, growing church. I would simply like to sharpen your discriminating abilities. Not everything the leaders of these churches—often with great assurance—promote as a panacea is really the right medicine for the rest of us.

Part 3

Six biotic principles

The key to the eight quality characteristics is the release of the "biotic potential" with which God has already endowed His church. If this is to become more than a nice theory, we must ask, "How does it work? What can we do to help the growth automatisms with which God Himself builds His church come into play more than they have so far?" If we follow the biblical example of learning from the laws inherent in God's creation and applying them to life within the kingdom of God, we encounter many principles which govern all of life—including the "organism" church.

Technocratic or biotic?

> **"Much of what has been published in the area of church growth comes closer to the 'robot' model than to the 'organism' model."**

The best symbol for what I have called "technocratic thinking" is a robot (see pictures in the left column). The more a guide to church growth resembles this kind of blueprint, the further it is removed from natural church development.

The biotic approach follows entirely different laws; it is the logic of life (see right column) versus the logic of machines. Regretfully, much of church growth literature in recent years comes closer in its thinking to the "robot" model than to the "organism" approach.

Why the "robot" model will not work

I am not implying that robot-making procedures do not work. They function very well indeed—in the world of technology, machines, and computers—in short, in the abiotic world. They fail miserably, however, in the biotic world. These are two fundamentally distinct areas, and it is futile to try to transfer methods developed in one of them into the other.

The technocratic approach: the "robot" model. From the beginning, all pieces are in their final form and are simply assembled according to a step-by-step plan. All end products are identical and do exactly what they have been programmed to do.

No one would ever think of sowing robots and waiting for them to germinate. We can't plant them, water them, or harvest them. We can't give them milk to help them grow, nor put them under a cold shower to strengthen their immune systems. The laws of organic growth do not apply in their world. Conversely, the technocratic principles of the world of robots do not apply in the world of life. We cannot expect them to help the living organism called "the church."

Technocratic church growth thinking is to natural church development as a robot is to

Photos 1-9 from: Frederic Vester, Unsere Welt – ein vernetztes System
© Deutscher Taschenbuch Verlag, Munich

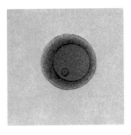

a human being, a model from the wax museum to the living original, a plastic flower to a fragrant rose. There is a certain resemblance, but it is no more then the superficial similarity between the series of pictures on these two pages.

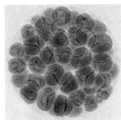

The biggest flaw in technocratic thinking is its total neglect of growth automatisms. No machine—not even the most ingenious robot—is able to reproduce itself. The "all by itself" principle that can be observed in all organic growth processes is unknown in the world of technology. Yet it is the key for understanding organic processes and particularly for understanding the organism "church."

In this chapter therefore, I want to describe certain principles which are typical for the biotic world. Even though they are all very different, they have one thing in common: they all help to bring about the greatest possible results with the least possible energy expenditure.

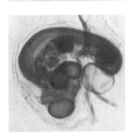

This efficient use of energy is one of the most interesting things we can observe among self-sustaining systems in God's creation. While in the world of technology a great amount of external energy is needed to set a machine in motion, in the world of life this happens "all by itself."

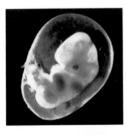

Blind to the "all by itself" principle

The biotic approach: the "organism" model. It is not made by assembling prefabricated pieces. A single cell begins to divide— first rapidly, later more slowly. In this way, a complex organism begins to develop. The outcome of this process is an individual with a distinct identity.

Why technocracy doesn't work

*"Technocratic
measures
frequently result
in the very op-
posite of what
was intended."*

We should never accuse Christians who tend towards tech-nocratic thinking of wrong motives. Their desire to protect the church of Jesus Christ is more than legitimate. We do not object to their *motives*, but to the *methods* with which they try to reach their goals.

To illustrate the shortsightedness of the technocratic approach, let's look at an example from a totally different area—wildlife management. In order to protect its elephant population, an African country established an elephant reservation. The short-range effect was a complete success: the elephant population, which had been kept small by natural enemies and diseases, was able to multiply unhindered. For a certain time, the supply of acacia trees was sufficient for the whole herd. But the more the herd increased, the more the vegetation was reduced by grazing. Eventually, the last acacia tree was grazed.

Now, conditions changed abruptly. Not only did multiplication stop; something much worse happened—the whole elephant herd died! The very measures intended to protect the elephants—which worked in the short run—led in the long run to their extinction (see picture).

Technocratic logic

The logic of the "elephant protectors" (which killed the elephants) is typical for technocratic thinking in general. It is the same logic that tells us that more traffic signs lead to greater

safety, newer weapons to more peace, stronger antibiotics to better health, higher welfare expenditures to less poverty, more fertilizer to higher yield. We now know—or at least should know—that this technocratic input-output logic is wrong in many cases.

As sensible as such measures may be in limited and time-bound situations, they all run the risk of destroying what they are meant to protect. An increase in traffic signs and regulations sometimes distracts drivers' attention, weapons can become the cause for conflicts, antibiotics weaken the immune system, welfare spending often dampens self-motivation, and fertilizers can poison the ground.

In many cases, such efforts cause long-term damage. The result is the very opposite of what was intended. This is because of the strictly linear logic of technocratic thinking ("from A to B") which we will describe in Part 4. Technocrats are blind to the circular repercussions of point B back onto point A. In order to understand natural processes, however, we need to have a grasp on these circular effects.

Blind to the repercussions

In churches, we see the same mistake that we encountered in the example of the elephants who were "protected to death" many times over. Let me mention one very typical example: a valued church worker resigns and the leadership tries to find a replacement. Since there seems to be no one with the same spiritual gifting, they decide to staff the position with a person willing to do the work—after all, "somebody has to do it." The immediate effect is very positive—the work continues, the new person feels honored by the request, and everybody seems content—at least for the time being.

The results of technocratic decisions

With a long-range perspective, however, it all looks different: the newcomer gets used to the idea that taking over a task which does not match one's spiritual gifts is normal. He might even interpret the frustration (that sets in because of a lack of giftedness) as "suffering for Christ," while his fellow church members compliment him for going beyond the call of duty. A false paradigm infects the church. Christians who might have the appropriate gifting are discouraged from volunteering for the job because it would seem rude to "push out" this dedicated servant of God!

This example might seem mundane, and yet it isn't. It is the end result of a chain of such technocratic decisions which leads to a step-by-step nullification of the "all by itself" principle in a church. Good intentions and human efforts increasingly supplant what God Himself wants to do.

Human strength instead of God's power

The following six principles are an attempt to relate the laws of the biotic world to our efforts in church development.

65

Principle 1:
Interdependence

"Whenever churches worked on one of the eight quality characteristics, the point value changed not only for that area, but for all other areas as well!"

Interdependence is the first of six "biotic principles" we will study with a view to their relationship to church growth. One of the great miracles of God's creation is the interdependence of its parts from the minutest microorganisms to the most magnificent stars. Our minds can hardly grasp the wisdom of this self-regulating system of interrelated elements. The biotic principle of interdependence states that the way the individual parts are integrated into a whole system is more important than the parts themselves.

This principle is fundamental for any form of church development, whether or not a congregation is aware of it. The church of Jesus Christ is a complex organism with many parts that are interrelated according to God's plan. It is virtually impossible to really understand any one of these parts (e.g., one of the eight "quality characteristics," or any church activity) until one has understood its relationship to the whole. If one acts upon any single element, it simultaneously affects all the other parts—a phenomenon foreign to linear thinking.

One cause, hundreds of effects

Our church surveys have enabled us to study first hand how this principle actually works. As a result of our research, we are able to provide any interested church with a quality index for each of the eight quality characteristics. With churches requesting repeated analyses, we have discovered an interesting fact: whenever they worked on one of the eight quality characteristics, the point value changed not only for that area, but for all other areas as well! Working on the quality characteristic "gift-oriented ministry," for example, has significant influence on other areas, including "leadership," "spirituality," "structures," and "relationships"— and those effects can be both positive and negative!

Interdependent thinking— interdependent structures

Interdependent thinking should result in interdependent church structures. However, not every form of interdependence is healthy, as can be seen in the illustrations on the right. It is essential to fashion a kind of interdependence that provides for the formation of sub-systems with a potential for ongoing multiplication. It is important that we draw inspiration from nature's blueprints—it is no accident that the Bible refers to them so often—instead of seeking

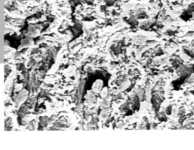

Well-ordered cells of normal intestinal mucous membrane (800:1)

Breakdown of the membrane structure caused by a fast growing carcinoma (800:1)

These illustrations show that by far not every kind of growth is positive (cf. the cancerous growth in the pictures right). A characteristic of healthy growth is "structured interdependence" (left), with clearly distinguishable sub-systems.

Structured interdependence

Unstructured interdependence

solutions to our planning problems in management books which in many cases are very technocratic in orientation.

While the *term* "interdependence" does not appear in the Bible—just like most other terms that I use in natural church development—the *reality* behind it is closely related to what is called "wisdom" in Scripture. To view a phenomenon in the context of its manifold relationships rather than in isolation, recognizing the order which God the Creator has intended—that is the basic nature of biblical wisdom. With this wisdom as our standard, the products of technocratic thinking may still come across as "intelligent," but certainly not as wise.

Interdependence and biblical wisdom

Church worker meetings

"The department heads of our church meet regularly for discussion"

80 %   78 %

25 %   29 %

high quality   growing
low quality   declining

Percentage of pastors who responded with "true" or "very true"

An example of "structured interdependence" within a church: Regular meetings of department heads. There is a highly significant difference between churches with high and churches with low quality indices.

Principle 2: Multiplication

"*A tree does not keep getting bigger; it brings forth new trees, which in turn produce more trees.*"

Unlimited growth, which might be a technocrat's dream, is profoundly unbiotic. Every form of organic growth sooner or later reaches its natural limits. A tree does not keep getting bigger; it brings forth new trees, which in turn produce more trees. This is the biotic principle of "multiplication," which characterizes all of God's creation.

Our research clearly shows how strongly this principle affects both the quality of a church and its growth. One example among many is the multiplication of small groups. We asked all survey participants whether their small group had the goal of multiplication by division. We purposely did not ask about the congregation's handling of small groups in general, but about concrete plans for their *own group*. The result, seen in the diagram below, is very revealing: Virtually no other aspect of church life has such an enormous influence on both the quality index and the growth of a church.

The true fruit of the apple tree

The principle of multiplication applies to all areas of church life: Just as the true fruit of an apple tree is not an apple, but another tree; the true fruit of a small group is not a new Christian, but another group; the true fruit of a church is not a new group, but a new church; the true fruit of a leader is not a follower, but a new leader; the true fruit of an evangelist is not a convert, but new evangelists. Whenever this principle is understood and applied, the results are dramatic—as can be shown empirically.

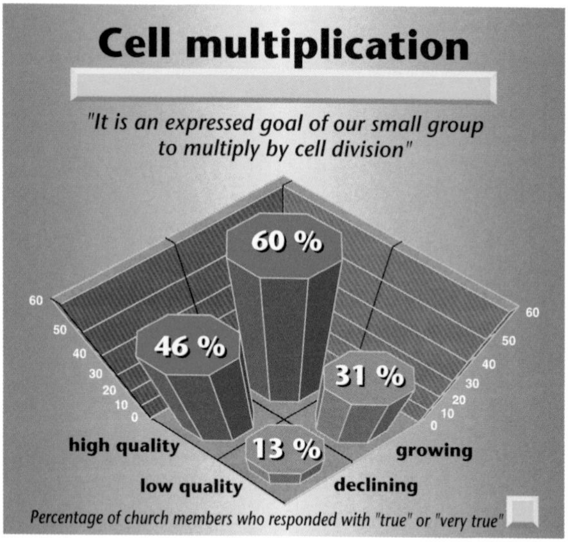

I believe that the concept of multiplication is by far the most important motive for planting new congregations, not antagonistic attitudes towards existing congregations, as some erroneously believe. Reproduction through multiplication is simply a life principle of all God-created organisms, including the church of Jesus Christ.

Cell multiplication

"It is an expressed goal of our small group to multiply by cell division"

60 %

46 %

31 %

13 %

high quality
low quality
growing
declining

Percentage of church members who responded with "true" or "very true"

Since we have shown (see pages 46-48) that it is not advisable for most churches to follow the megachurch model, the matter of church multiplication becomes even more important. Advocating small churches does not at all mean advocating stagnation at low attendance levels. It is an appeal for continual multiplication. Our study showed a clear positive correlation between the quality index of a church and the number of churches it had planted within the last five years.

Hardly anything demonstrates the health of a congregation as much as the willingness—and ability!—to give birth to new congregations. The opposite is true as well. Hardly anything is a more clear indication of illness than structures which by design hinder church multiplication, or at best permit it as an absolute exception.

The model of Christ's ministry

While the term "multiplication" is not found in the Bible, we can find many illustrations of how God uses this principle. The best example is the ministry of Christ. He invested Himself primarily in His twelve disciples, who in turn were commissioned to make disciples who would also make disciples. What is the Great Commission if not a call for ongoing multiplication?

Multiplication and death

Where multiplication processes are functioning, straightforward talk about "death" is also permitted. Why should groups or even whole churches not be allowed to die after they have run their course? This thought should not be threatening at all, if the given church or group has produced four "children," 16 "grandchildren," and 54 "great-grandchildren!" In God's creation, the "genetic information" remains and reproduces itself, though individual organisms may die.

Principle 3:
Energy transformation

*"It seems to me
that this is one
of the least-
known church
growth prin-
ciples of all."*

One of nature's principal ways of guaranteeing the survival of organisms and whole ecological systems is what ecology calls the "jiu-jitsu principle." Existing forces and energies—even hostile energies—are turned in the desired direction through minute steering energies. Thus destructive energy can become product-ive. The opposite of this principle would be a "boxer's mentality" of first, using force to annihilate the opponent's (or the environ-ment's) strength and then using force again to reach the in-tended goal.

We can study the principle of *energy transformation* by observing how an organism fights a virus. Viruses generally make us sick, therefore they are bad. A few viruses, however, cause the body to counteract and strengthen its immune system. This is the prin-ciple used in vaccinations. Health-destroying energies are transfor-med through the vaccination process into health-promoting ones.

How God uses this principle

We frequently encounter the principle of energy transformation in Scripture. One of the most famous examples is the way Paul, on the Areopagus, referred to the "unknown god" (obviously an idol) and made it the point of departure for his evangelistic sermon in Athens (Acts 17). God's use through the ages of the persecution of Christians (Acts 8) to advance the Gospel is another variation on this principle. The blood of martyrs becomes the seed of the church. "Hostile energy" is thus transformed into "holy energy."

Using crises creatively

Understanding this principle has far-reaching consequences that influence even how crises and catastrophes are handled. One must neither passively yield to fate ("God has brought it about") nor obstinately protest against it ("Satan did it"), but rather ask oneself, "How can I best use this situation for the advance of God's kingdom?" This is a very creative question—and it is also biblical. The promise in Romans 8:28 reads, "And we know that God causes all things to work together for good to those who love God."

It seems to me that this is probably one of the least-known church growth principles of all, yet its consistent application could help churches in crisis more enduringly than many popular growth gimmicks.

A surfer is a good illustration of the principle of energy transformation. Instead of wasting energy fighting the waves ("boxer mentality"), he utilizes the power of the waves through skillful steering.

Consequences for evangelism

Many technocratic forms of ministry—such as manipulative methods in evangelism—have a close affinity to the boxer mentality. A need-oriented approach is totally different. Here the needs of non-Christians (and these are not necessarily "spiritual" needs at all!) are taken seriously, and the energy behind them is made to serve God's purposes for these people.

Churches with high quality indices instinctively understand the importance of this principle, as seen, for example, in the way they involve new converts in evangelism (see chart right). Many churches hesitate to include these new Christians in evangelistic efforts, because of their spiritual immaturity and lack of knowledge (they might say something wrong). The principle of energy transformation, however, sees the possibilities: new converts still have many contacts to "the world," still speak the "worldly" language, and have many thought patterns in common with their non-Christian friends. Instead of crying "Danger! Look out!" growing churches use these energies for the kingdom of God.

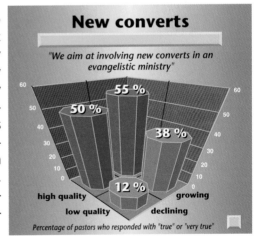

New converts

"We aim at involving new converts in an evangelistic ministry"

55 %

50 %

38 %

12 %

high quality   growing

low quality   declining

Percentage of pastors who responded with "true" or "very true"

Principle 4:
Multi-usage

"The multi-usage principle is the best therapy for countless multi-burdened Christians."

The biotic principle of multi-usage is best illustrated by the picture on the right. The leaves that fall off the tree are by no means "waste" whose disposal will cost extra energy (typical technocratic logic). Microorganisms in the soil transform dead leaves into humus, which in turn provides important nutrients for the further growth of the tree and the production of new foliage. Such cycles are a basic structure of all forms of life. To the extent that we succeed in setting up similar processes in our churches, we also will experience how energy, once invested, can be put to many uses.

It seems to me that this principle has often been understood simplistically. While it certainly makes sense for church facilities to be multi-purpose, or for the pastor's sermon preparation to double as Bible study notes, these do not capture the full meaning behind the term multi-usage. As we observed in the example of the tree, the point of the principle is that the results of work are transformed into energy, which in turn sustains the ongoing work.

Multi-usage and discipleship

The essential meaning of multi-usage is well illustrated by the principle of co-leadership, which is used much more in churches with a high quality index than in others (diagram left). These churches do not have, on the one hand, leaders who invest their energies in leadership only, and on the other hand, training programs to develop new leaders. Instead, actual participation in leadership provides the best training for new leaders. The initial energy investment is put to multiple use, and ultimately serves towards recruiting new leaders.

This is precisely the model we observe in the ministry of Christ. He did not have separate programs for discipleship training and public ministry. He trained His dis-

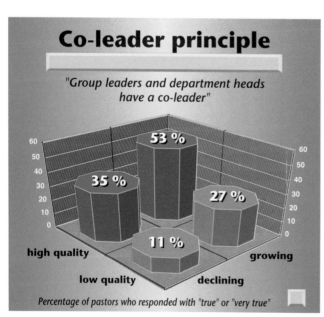

Co-leader principle

"Group leaders and department heads have a co-leader"

53 %

35 %

27 %

11 %

high quality

low quality

growing

declining

Percentage of pastors who responded with "true" or "very true"

There is no "waste" in nature: Leaves that fall from a tree turn into humus and provide nutrients to support the further growth of the tree from which they fell.

ciples by ministering to people. This on-the-job experience yields higher-quality training with a smaller investment of energy.

Financial self-organization

The multi-usage principle affects all areas of church life, including the finances. A typical example of the linear logic of the technocratic paradigm is the classical "donor model" (which without a doubt is justified in certain situations). Let's assume that a donor (point A) supports some project (point B). Results from the project have no direct effect on the source (i.e., the donor, or point A). Represented graphically, we envision an arrow from A to B. This process requires a twofold energy expense: first, attending to the donors, and second, completing the project. Energy spent on the former is obviously lost to the latter—multi-burden rather than multi-usage!

By contrast, in the cyclical model those benefiting from the project (point B) contribute to its financing (point A). The energy has come full circle. The same energy that is spent working on the project provides its financial backing. Thus a financially self-supporting structure develops.

73

Principle 5: Symbiosis

"It is a tragedy that for many Christians the ideal of unity has often been married to the concept of a monopolistic system."

Symbiosis, according to Webster, is "the intimate living together of two dissimilar organisms in a mutually beneficial relationship." Two negative models stand in contrast to this principle: *competition* and *monoculture*. Competition assumes "dissimilar organisms," just like symbiosis does, but these organisms harm rather than help one another. Monoculture, on the other hand (called monopolism in economics and society), has lost the variety of species, and one type of organism dominates. This obviously eliminates destructive competition, but it also takes away the symbiotic interdependence of different species.

Every form of monoculture is an expression of technocratic thinking. Technocrats are blind to the important, stabilizing effects of hedges, swamps, and horticultural variety. Today we know that optimal agriculture—like all organic systems—requires plant diversity. Overblown attempts to increase efficiency by monocultural planting destroy the free self-regulation provided by symbiosis and natural interdependence. In the long run, the entire ecosystem is badly damaged (see pictures top right). The less we profit from the free performance of intact ecological systems, the more energy we have to pump into agriculture. We try to compensate through artificial fertilizers and pesticides for what nature would otherwise regulate "all by itself."

Unity does not mean monopoly

It is a tragedy that for many Christians the ideal of unity has often been married to the concept of a monopolistic system—a typical expression of technocratic thinking. For them, Christian unity is the greatest when all churches belong to a single large denomination, employ the same liturgy, and hold to the same practices. The parallels to monocultural farming are as easily seen as the technocratic thinking behind both models.

Spiritual gifts and symbiosis

In our research we were able to observe the fruitfulness of symbiotic cooperation in many different areas of church life. Probably the best example is the gift-oriented approach to ministry. Instead of producing carbon-copy Christian workers, the church encourages the interplay of widely diverse gifts and personality types, all benefiting one another. A typical result of working with such symbiotic structures is that the needs of individual Christians

Monoculture of lettuce

Erosion caused by excessive monoculture

("What do I enjoy?") and the needs of the congregation ("What will help our church grow?") complement rather than compete with one another. In any event, it is striking that churches with a high quality index apply this principle more consistently than others (see diagram below).

Current secular management literature refs to this principle as "win-win relationships." This means that rather than having winners and losers, decisions are made in such a way that everybody wins. Though some management theorists celebrate this as a novelty, it is really not unlike the "Golden Rule" which Jesus taught 2000 years ago. He certainly did not call it "win-win" or symbiosis, but "loving your neighbor."

The "Golden Rule"

If we had to choose between competition or monopoly, there is no question that I would prefer competition. As undesirable as it may be, the competitive model is a tremendous improvement on the obtuseness, monotony, and ineffectiveness of monopolism. The good news is that as Christians we are not limited to these two alternatives. The spiritual principle of symbiosis surpasses both other approaches by far!

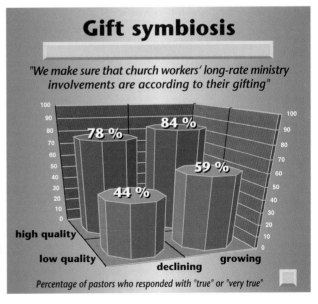

Gift symbiosis

"We make sure that church workers' long-rate ministry involvements are according to their gifting"

78 %
84 %
59 %
44 %

high quality

low quality

declining

growing

Percentage of pastors who responded with "true" or "very true"

Principle 6: Functionality

"All living things in God's creation are characterized by the ability to bear fruit."

Every detail in God's creation has a specific function. This is true even when the function may not be apparent at first glance. Why, for instance, are rivers so winding? Or what is the good of an insect? When technocrats are unable to discern the unique natural function, they proceed with corrective measures such as straightening rivers or spraying pesticides. This is done in the name of "functionalism" (a favorite term of technocrats), but what they mean is the functionality of a robot, not the biotic, self-regulating functionality which will be discussed in this chapter.

All living things in God's creation are characterized by their ability to bear fruit. Inherent to the nature of this fruit—be it an apple, a chestnut, or even a baby—is the preservation of the species. Where there is no fruit, life is condemned to death.

"Fruit" in the Bible

It is no accident that Jesus repeatedly referred to this natural law and applied it to the spiritual realm. In Matthew 7 we read, "Every good tree bears good fruit" and "You will know them by their fruits" (verses 17 and 16). Since fruit—according to both biology and the Bible—is visible, we are able to check on the quality of an organism (or church) by examining its fruit.

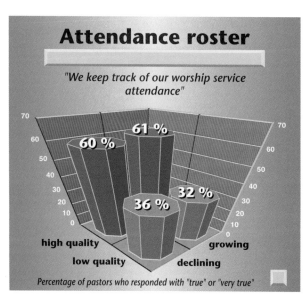

Attendance roster

"We keep track of our worship service attendance"

61 %

60 %

32 %

36 %

high quality   growing

low quality   declining

Percentage of pastors who responded with "true" or "very true"

Natural church development has two levels of questions about fruit. One level is quality: How high is the quality index of the eight quality characteristics for a specific church? The other level is quantity: Is the church growing or multiplying? It is significant that such questions are usually not even asked in churches with a low quality index (see diagram left).

This kind of "success check" is important in order to protect the principle-oriented approach from ideological misuse. We have already seen that in natural church development, in contrast to pragmatism, indi-

Both in the literal and in the figurative sense, all of nature is designed to bear fruit. Where no fruit appears, something is wrong.

vidual decisions should not be made by asking, "Is this useful (for increased worship attendance) or not?" Instead, we should ask: "Does this decision agree with the fundamental church growth principles?" A good way to evaluate whether our ministry is *really* in harmony with these principles of church development is to periodically examine our visible fruit.

Lamentably, the criterion of functionality is considered unspiritual in many Christian circles. Yet it is noteworthy how frequently Scripture addresses this topic. In the New Testament alone, the word "useful" appears 19 times. The key to understanding biblical "usefulness" is found in 1 Corinthians 10:23. It reads, "All things are lawful, but not all things are useful. All things are lawful, but not all things edify."

"Usefulness" in the Bible

This evidently means that what is useful, is that which edifies. The word "edifies" is translated from *oikodomeo*, one of the key words in church development. "Edification" in its biblical sense is not just "edifying feelings," but is a word borrowed from architecture, specifically describing the building up of the church of Jesus Christ.

Biotic = the opposite of the usual

"The principles of natural church development are pretty much the opposite of what most churches 'normally' consider to be right."

What exactly makes each of the eight quality characteristics described in Part 1 "biotic?"

Notice the chart to the right which separates the nouns and adjectives of each characteristic. The secret of the eight quality characteristics lies not in the nouns (e.g., leadership, ministry, spirituality), but in the adjectives (e.g., empowering, gift-oriented, passionate). While what the nouns represent exists in virtually every church, the secret of churches with a high quality index is their ability to make room for God's growth automatisms in all areas. How does this happen? Through the—conscious or unconscious—application of the biotic principles described in this chapter.

In church growth literature there are numerous lists of "characteristics of growing churches." To date, I have collected 23 such lists from different authors, and they are all fairly similar. The reason I prefer "our" list to others is that the biotic "secret of success" of each quality characteristic is unmistakably expressed through the adjectives.

The terminology may seem relatively abstract, but that lies in the nature of this subject. One single term must cover a whole array of possible situations, which vary greatly from one church to another, though following a common blueprint.

The source of opposition

Several years ago, when we began developing materials designed to aid churches in the practical implementation of the biotic approach, we made an interesting discovery. The principles of natural church development are pretty much the *opposite* of what most churches normally consider to be right.

In practice (not in their official teaching), some churches earnestly defend as particularly "spiritual" a style of ministry which reflects the opposite of our quality adjectives. Whenever natural church development is implemented, the stubborn persistence of what we have called the "spiritualistic" and "technocratic" paradigms in "normal" Christian thinking becomes palpable.

The reason for low quality

Our research revealed that the release of God's growth automatisms is the "secret of success" for churches with a high quality

Biotic element (Release of the "all by itself" principle)	Ministry area	Part 3: 6 biotic principles
Empowering	leadership	
Gift-oriented	ministry	
Passionate	spirituality	
Functional	structures	
Inspiring	worship service	
Holistic	small groups	
Need-oriented	evangelism	
Loving	relationships	

A chart of the eight quality characteristics: While the areas of ministry (right column) exist in virtually every church, the secret of growing churches is their ability to follow the "all by itself" principle in every single area (left column).

index—regardless of the way they themselves explained their growth.

This statement has an important reciprocal: If churches have a low quality index and are struggling to grow, it is because they are doing something wrong. It is clear that they are *not* applying the biotic principles described in this chapter. It is almost always possible to pinpoint the problem in a church with a low quality index. What isn't so easy, however, is to change the situation for the better.

I certainly do not want to suggest that crowds of people will suddenly flock to our churches as soon as we apply biotic principles. The Gospel is sometimes rejected because of the message of the cross itself. On the other hand, *some* obstacles are erected by God's "ground troops" using faulty methods. As long as we turn the principles of church development upside down in our churches, we should be very careful about attributing our lack of success solely to the message of the cross.

False paradigms, false methods

Learning to think biotically

"The six biotic principles tell us not only how to act, but also how to creatively react in a way that supports growth."

Hopefully by now it has become clear why natural church development does not offer a prefabricated program, but concentrates on the transmission of principles. Our approach differs from a legalistic ideology ("We must follow this program point for point") and from a pragmatism without principles ("The end justifies the means"). The chart to the right illustrates the differences between the approaches.

Most people, including pastors, are not used to integrated thinking. Based on my experience however, "biotic thinking" can be learned. When I am invited to speak at a pastors' seminar on natural church development, my goal is not for every participant to leave with a list of pat answers—notwithstanding the expectations of some pastors. My aim is to expose the traps in our normal "Christian" thought structures and help people "think biotically." Using case studies, we try to spell out what the application of biotic principles could mean for the everyday life of various churches.

When someone describes a situation to me and asks what should be done, I usually do not answer, but ask in return, "What could applying the biotic principle of energy transformation (or multiplication or symbiosis) mean in this situation?" Then we discuss the issue together and are often amazed at how many creative solutions can be stimulated by this simple question. To use an analogy: rather than offering "cut flowers," I want to help churches grow their own. I am convinced that this approach is helpful in other areas as well.

Principles and intuition

In these group activities, I have noticed that our intuition over and again misleads us to make abiotic rather than biotic decisions. Only after we have worked with this approach for some time, our intuition will gradually change. Then we will no longer need to rely on the six principles for help; we will *intuitively* make the right decisions. It all depends on what shapes our intuition!

The value of the six biotic principles for everyday church life is that they tell us not only how to *act*, but also how to creatively *react* in a way that supports growth. More than 90 percent of pastors' work involves reacting to situations that are not of their

	Ideological approach	Pragmatic approach	Principle-oriented approach	*Part 3:* *6 biotic* *principles*
Key question	"Which ready-made pro-gram should I use?"	"What is most useful in this situation?"	"What do the biblical prin-ciples mean in this situa-tion?"	
Creed	"We must go by laws which were estab-lished once and for all"	"There are no universal principles—the end justi-fies the means"	"Growth prin-ciples need to be newly cus-tomized for each changing situation"	
Result	No growth (this condition is interpreted as proof of loyal obedi-ence)	Artificial growth (through human wis-dom)	Natural growth (in harmony with God's growth prin-ciples)	*This chart shows how the principle-oriented approach differs from both the ideological and pragmatic approach.*

own choosing: the marriage of a church worker falls apart; there is a financial bottleneck; building repairs have to be made; one of the elders resigns; a church member feels neglected; the pastor has trouble harmonizing ministry and personal matters.
Natural church development cannot exclude such problems from church growth, but tries to help leaders make everyday de-cisions in alignment with God's growth automatisms. The sum of these daily decisions constitutes practical church development—not just pastors brooding over bombastic church growth goals.

Bringing it down to the essentials

A diligent student of the six biotic principles will notice that they are all variations of one single principle: "How can we create an environment that will allow God's growth automatisms—with which He Himself builds the church—ever-increasing influence?" Ultimately all church growth principles can be reduced to this question. During the last few years, I have learned that it is not important to know hundreds of intricate principles—what matters is to develop a "sense" (even if somewhat vague or un-defined) for how God's growth automatisms work.

Not more
work—relief!
What we have said thus far about the achievement levels within church life is not an abstract theory. It makes a big difference—even on the emotional level—whether pastors push and shove a congregation in their own strength, or whether they concentrate on letting God's growth mechanisms take hold in their churches. Church workers in congregations with a high quality index have demonstrably more joy in their ministry and feel less overworked. They experience what it means to have the Holy Spirit build the church.

Of course there are high-quality-index churches with overworked members—too many, in fact. However, being overworked is not a church growth principle—as some make it out to be—but a *flaw* that is sometimes found in an otherwise healthy con-gregation. We should beware of trying to make success principles out of mistakes that happen to accompany a church's success.

How
"accidents"
happen
When we look at growing churches, it sometimes seems as if many good things just happen to them—be it by accident or because of God's blessing—and this is often how these churches perceive their own situation. In reality they have gained a differ-ent perspective on the challenges facing them. They have learned that certain problems (which for some are hidden and for others are a hindrance) are opportunities to be used creatively for the kingdom of God.

This is the kind of vision we hope to gain by adopting the six biotic principles.

A new paradigm

Natural church development is not just one church growth method among many. It is a different theological paradigm altogether. It introduces a different way of thinking for Christians. Throughout this book, we have encountered traces of what we have called the "technocratic" and "spiritualistic" paradigms. What are the backgrounds of these different thought patterns? A grasp of them will, among other things, help us understand the opposition which is likely to arise when natural church development is implemented.

Bipolarity in the Bible

Polarity is an ubiquitous phenomenon in God's creation. We are probably most familiar with the polarity in the human brain. The left half of the brain—which controls the *right* side of the body—is known for its capacity for rational thinking, logic, and speech. The right half—which controls the *left* side of the body—is the artistic half; it sees and stores images, remembers melodies, creates poetry. It is the intuitive, creative side. Similar polar interaction can be found throughout creation, for instance, in electricity, magnetism, or in the relationship between husband and wife, to name but a few.

The law of polarity states that for every force there must be a counterforce. The relationship of the two poles causes a flow of energy, which directly influences what we have described as the "principle of self-organization."

Consider the polarity of genders for example. Human reproduction does not need artificial promptings—it happens *all by itself,* simply through the mutual attraction of the "poles."

Bipolar thinking in the Bible

We find the same kind of bipolarity in the New Testament, where the church is referred to with both dynamic and static images. Typical *dynamic* images describe the church with organic metaphors (for example, the church as a "body" as in Romans 12:4-8). Other texts use *static* images borrowed from the world of architecture and construction (for example, Paul as the wise architect who has laid a foundation for others to build upon in 1 Corinthians 3:10).

In this context, the term "static pole" has no negative connotations, but refers to the concept of static as it is used in architecture, simply meaning "a basic necessity for any good building."

Several sections of the New Testament even combine dynamic and

	Dynamic pole: organic	**Static pole: technical**
1 Pet. 2:5	*"living...*	*stones"*
Eph. 2:21	*"growth...*	*of the temple"*
Eph. 4:12	*"body of Christ...*	*built"*
1 Cor. 3:9	*"God's field and...*	*God's building"*

The bipolar church concept

Dynamic and static pole

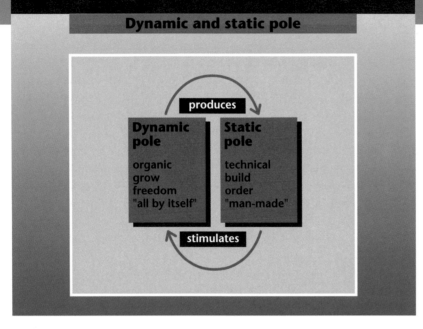

*The bipolar
church concept:
Static and dyna-
mic poles, organ-
ism and organi-
zation are inter-
related and inter-
acting.*

static images, at times seeming to create mutually exclusive pictures (see diagram on the bottom left hand page). It is characteristic of biblical thinking to have both poles represented, and one
does not rule out the other.

The illustration above shows that the two poles are in a reciprocal
relationship. The dynamic pole always creates organization
(structures, institutions, rules, or programs). The purpose of this
organization is, in its turn, to develop further the dynamic pole.
As long as this cycle is intact—in practice, not just in our thinking—there is a highly creative relationship between the two
poles. It can be demonstrated that churches where this is evident
are typically healthy and growing.

**It's circulation
that matters!**

The circle in the picture above represents the work of the Holy
Spirit. It is also symbolic of the release of the "biotic potential"
resulting from the creative interaction between the two poles.
The Holy Spirit causes the growth. The problem is that in most
churches the cycle has broken down. In such cases, the bipolar
paradigm is replaced by one-dimensional thinking, causing the
false paradigms often mentioned in this book.

Dangers to the right and to the left

*"Most Chris-
tians think
either dualisti-
cally or monisti-
cally, spiritua-
listically or
technocratically.
That's a
problem."*

The cycle connecting the dynamic and static poles—as illustrated to the right—can break down in two ways.

It is possible, for instance, to take the right (institutional) pole and treat it as the whole, presuming that where this pole exists, the church of Jesus Christ is present in its fullness. I call this view "monism." It is the thought structure of the technocratic paradigm. Monism treats both poles as one. People who are influenced by this thought pattern are convinced that if only the right pole has the right form (right doctrine, right political persuasion, right church growth program, etc.), then they don't have to worry about the left pole (the dynamic life of the organism called the church).

The cycle can also break down on the left. In this case, the dynamic pole is separated from its static counterpart. Forms, programs, structures, and institutions are considered spiritually irrelevant, perhaps even harmful. I call this view "dualism." It represents the thought structure of what we have described in this book as the spiritualistic paradigm.

What do "monism" and "dualism" mean?

An illustration may help clarify these somewhat abstract terms. To hear music from stereo equipment requires two poles, two loudspeakers. A monistic approach in this context would be like listening to a recording in a reduced "mono" mode, claiming that the music is terrific and fully convinced that the one loudspeaker reflects "the whole."

On the other hand, dualistic thinking would be like insisting that only the left loudspeaker is ever needed, because the right speaker is unnecessary for enjoying the wonderful music, and might even be dangerous. The truth of the matter is that God has given us two ears—another bipolarity in His creation—and thus the way we enjoy music must take this bipolarity into account.

This illustration shows us that the two positions are in one sense quite different: monism treats both poles as one, dualism disconnects the two poles. But they have one thing in common, however: they are both incapable of a bipolar view. Monistic thinking in church growth leads easily to technocratic approaches ("Follow this program, and your church will grow"). Dualistic think-

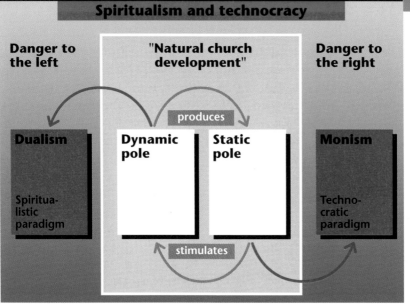

Dangers to the right and to the left

Spiritualism and technocracy

Danger to the left

"Natural church development"

Danger to the right

produces

Dualism

Dynamic pole

Static pole

Monism

Spiritualistic paradigm

Technocratic paradigm

stimulates

Natural church development and its dangers to the left and to the right. While monism treats both poles as one, dualism disconnects them.

ing, on the other hand, often produces an anti-institutional spiritualism ("Institutions are spiritually irrelevant"). Both are far removed from the reality God the Creator has placed in humanity; both impede biblical thinking; both hinder living faith—and both frustrate efforts to seek church growth and development as well.

Different paradigms work like differently tinted glasses. You and I may look at the same evidence (either in or outside the church), we may even read the same verse of Scripture, and yet see entirely different realities. The problem with both dualistic and monistic thinking is that they blind us in one eye or the other. With these handicaps, try as we may, we cannot discern the full picture!

Paradigms are like glasses

Most Christians think either dualistically or monistically, spiritualistically or technocratically. They are unable to "see" the bipolar position unless they receive the necessary "glasses" to help them. That's why it makes sense for us to take a closer look at the two "false" paradigms we are dealing with. This should help explain the source of the resistance to the bipolar, biotic, and also biblical approach to church life and ministry.

The technocratic paradigm

"The psycho-
logical root of
the technocratic
paradigm is a
widespread
security
mentality."

Let us now consider the character of the technocratic paradigm. When technocrats look at churches, they typically only notice the right pole, the institutional side. They tend to believe that attending to a church's institutional needs will automatically yield the elements symbolized by the left pole.

Technocratic thinking may assume widely diverse forms. Let me give some examples:

- "Once ordained, a pastor is automatically endowed with all spiritual authority for ministry."

- "Celebrate your services in this way, and the Holy Spirit will automatically descend upon your congregation."

- "Accept this teaching, and you will automatically be a true Christian."

- "Use this church growth program, and your church will automatically grow."

Varieties of technocratic thinking

All of these examples cover a broad spectrum of opinions and theological persuasions—from clericalism to sacralism, from dogmatism to church growth technocracy. Although in sharp disagreement with one another, they have in common the technocratic thought pattern which presumes that attending to the institutional (right) pole will guarantee the dynamics of the left pole.

Trusting in this kind of automatism keeps a technocrat from perceiving that the two poles are different and distinct. Technocrats cannot really see the dissimilarities between being ordained and receiving spiritual gifts, between attending a church service and experiencing the presence of the Holy Spirit, between accepting certain dogmas and having a personal relationship to Christ, between pushing a church growth program and experiencing vibrant church life.

A concept of simple cause and effect

Faith in this kind of automatism has absolutely nothing in common with the biotic automatisms described in this book (see pages 12-13). Instead, this automatism resembles that of a vend-

The technocratic paradigm

The error of monistic thinking

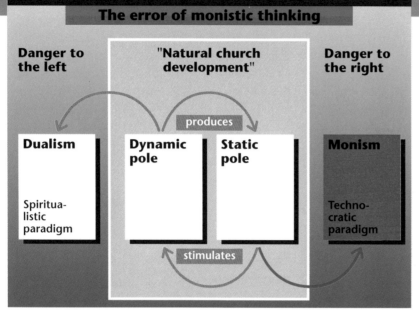

Danger to the left	"Natural church development"		Danger to the right

produces

Dualism	Dynamic pole	Static pole	Monism
Spiritua-listic paradigm			Techno-cratic paradigm

stimulates

A look at the technocratic paradigm: Monistic thinking does not differentiate between the two poles in the center. This view in effect absolutizes the right pole.

ing machine. Its static cause-effect design looks something like this: Insert coin, take out Coke.

Indeed, the technocratic paradigm comes close to magical thinking. In the same way that a magician utters the magic words "abracadabra" to bring about the desired results—automatically, irresistibly, and with absolute certainty—so technocrats are utterly convinced that their formulas, dogmas, institutions, or church growth programs will have a similar magical effect.

The psychological force behind the technocratic paradigm is a "security mentality," which is widespread even among Christians. Rather than trusting in the person of Christ alone, people look for some form of outward security. It isn't enough for them to create institutions that *stimulate* the organic pole of the church. They look for programs that will *guarantee* its health.

Monistic-technocratic thinking is, at least in Western churches, the most widespread paradigm. It is their greatest liability—by the second generation if not sooner. Paradoxically, the *intentions* of people in these churches are in many cases good and spiritually motivated. Nevertheless, it can be shown how much this paradigm harms the organism church.

The security mentality

The spiritualistic paradigm

> *"A spiritualist considers institutional elements second-rate, or in the worst case, downright evil."*

The dualism behind the spiritualistic paradigm manifests itself on different levels. It is a dualism between spirit and matter, organism and organization, God's work and human labor, the supernatural and the natural. Dualism means that the poles are viewed as opposing, rather than correlated elements. Only the dynamic pole is considered to be "spiritual"; the institutional elements are seen as second-rate, or in the worst case, as downright evil.

Spiritualism should be understood as a reaction against the technocratic paradigm. Its inherent weakness is not in its denunciation of the technocratic view of institutions, but in its attempt to do away with institutions altogether. This reveals its greatest defect, a damaged relationship to creation itself. Spiritualists do not understand that God Himself gave all that He had created the label "very good" (Genesis 1:31). They do not understand that incarnation means that "the Word became flesh" (John 1:14). They do not understand that the Spirit of God is the Maker and Sustainer of creation (Psalm 104:30, Job 34:13-15). Creation means: God breathes His Spirit into dead matter.

A gnostic view of the Holy Spirit

Spiritualistically inclined people often do sound very "spiritual" indeed. Upon closer examination, however, they reveal a closer proximity to gnosticism than to Scripture.

Don't let me be misunderstood. I am not suggesting that Christians leaning towards a spiritualistic paradigm necessarily support gnostic theology. More often than not they adhere to very orthodox *doctrine*, confessing God as Creator, the incarnation of the Son, and the Holy Spirit as the One who builds the church. And yet, their subconscious, their intuitions, and their emotions reflect an understanding of the world and of the Holy Spirit which is essentially gnostic, and this hidden realm has a much greater influence on practical ministry than officially sanctioned doctrine.

About rules and exceptions to the rules

In speaking to groups that are marked by the spiritualistic paradigm, I encounter the same situation over and over again. Whatever I share about the principles our research has revealed, i.e., how God "normally" works in and through churches, is dis-

The spiritualistic paradigm

The error of dualistic thinking

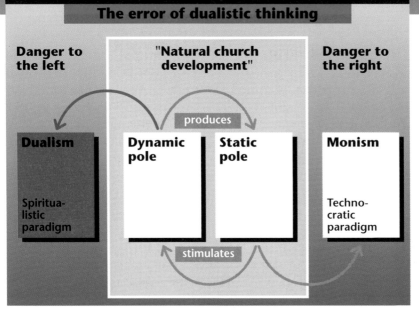

Danger to the left

"Natural church development"

Danger to the right

produces

Dualism

Spiritualistic paradigm

Dynamic pole

Static pole

Monism

Technocratic paradigm

stimulates

A look at the spiritualistic paradigm: Spiritualistic thinking is not only at odds with a technocratic view of institutions, it opposes all institutional issues.

counted by some listeners as almost "unspiritual" or "hardly edifying." As soon as I mention some exceptions to the rule—which are strategically and spiritually much less weighty—their eyes get that sparkle, as if they wanted to say: "Now, there is truly God at work!"

Normally one should live by the rule rather than by the exception to the rule. But just what is "normal?" The attitudes described above (all rules and principles are suspect) are consistent within the spiritualistic paradigm. If the rules and principles we are describing are unspiritual, then it is only through breaking them that the Holy Spirit works.

God's work or human's?

In the logic of the spiritualistic paradigm, the clear, unequivocal influence of the Holy Spirit is particularly evident when God does not make use of programs, institutions, planning, or management in building a church. Dualistic thinkers cannot see the incongruity of God constantly breaking His own rules of life in order to build His church. For them, the principles described in this book are not made by God, but by humans, or perhaps even by Satan. This view makes sense—but only within a framework of spiritualistic presuppositions.

The effect of wrong paradigms

"Spiritualists and technocrats cannot even see the bipolar position."

Once we have seriously tried to understand the spiritualistic and technocratic paradigms from the inside, it is almost impossible not to sympathize to some extent with *both*. Spiritualists, as we have seen, battle valiantly against rationalism, false security, and the technocratic "can-do" mentality. Who would not agree with them, except perhaps the technocrats themselves? When it comes to fighting these issues, I side with the spiritualists.

On the other hand, technocrats vehemently oppose the irrationality and the nebulous "other-worldliness" of the spiritualistic paradigm. Once again we must admit that they have a legitimate case—biblically, theologically, and strategically. This appears very confusing, at least at first glance. Can both the spiritualists and the technocrats be right? How can we agree with both views precisely in those areas in which they contradict each other?

Blind to the bipolar view

To solve this problem, we must understand how the bipolar paradigm of natural church development is seen from each of the two extremes: *it is not seen at all* (see graphic)! Since spiritualists and technocrats both have an "either-or" position, they cannot perceive the middle area.

When *spiritualists*, for example, look at the bipolar approach, they cannot distinguish it from the technocratic view, because they are against institutions as a matter of principle. They cannot distinguish between a strictly functional view of institutions (typical of the bipolar paradigm) and the gross overestimation of institutions (typical of the technocratic paradigm). For them, it is all the same: a spiritually questionable contract with institutions.

And how do *technocrats* perceive natural church development? From their perspective, it is a campaign against all institutional, technical, rational and program-oriented aspects of church growth. Or, if technocrats are not proponents of the church growth movement (and there are a lot of this kind, too), they might view natural church development as a campaign against all forms, traditions, and rites.

Why we don't understand each other

I am often mistaken for being either a spiritualist or a technocrat, depending on which of the camps I am visiting. For many years I wondered, "Why am I seen as a perpetrator of the very things

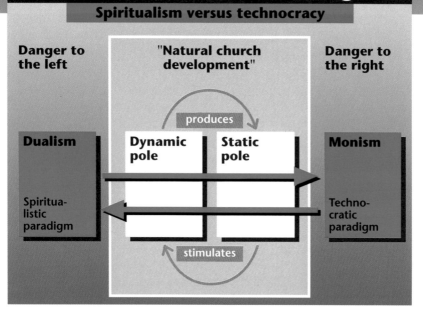

The consequences of one-dimensional thinking

Spiritualism versus technocracy

Danger to the left	"Natural church development"		Danger to the right
Dualism	**Dynamic pole**	**Static pole**	**Monism**
Spiritua-listic paradigm	produces / stimulates		Techno-cratic paradigm

The clash between the spiritualistic and the technocratic paradigms has its root in their inability to perceive the middle position.

I oppose?" More often than not I would respond with surprise, "Weren't you listening? Just tell me one sentence that substantiates your suspicions." Within *my own* paradigm, I was right. What I didn't understand was that the suspicions were fully consistent within the paradigms of my critics. Different paradigms are incompatible.

A mental revolution

From their own point of view, both spiritualists and technocrats are consistent in identifying the bipolar position with their rival stereotype. The first time this truth dawned on me, it was a virtual breakthrough. Suddenly I realized why so many discussions on church growth issues are so unproductive. They simply cannot be productive as long as we are operating from different paradigms. Neither side can hear what the other is saying.

What we need is no less than a "mental revolution." I intentionally do not say "spiritual revolution," because the root problems are frequently not found in that arena, as we have shown. The real problem lies in the different patterns of thinking (i.e., different paradigms) with which we categorize and interpret our spiritual experiences.

Theological consequences

The incompatibility of the thinking behind the different paradigms mentioned above shows up in nearly every theological issue. In my book *Paradigmenwechsel in der Kirche* (Paradigm Shift in the Church), I try to demonstrate that in the last analysis almost all major conflicts in church history, right up to the most controversial issues in the church today, can be explained as a struggle between monism and dualism, objectivism and subjectivism, heteronomism and autonomism, between technocracy and spiritualism. In other words, they are conflicts between two misunderstandings of the Christian faith! Unless we have a paradigm shift, we will struggle with these conflicts until Christ's return.

An abbreviated presentation of my research into church history is illustrated to the right. A list of the typical "-isms" which continually appear in theological discussions is displayed under the dualistic and the monistic paradigms. Note that monism, the thought pattern of the technocratic paradigm, appears in many different forms, whether as technocratic church growth thinking, sacramentalism, or clericalism. All of these are only different varieties of the same monistic thought pattern.

**The
"reformation
principle"**

Upon closer examination of the chart to the right, it becomes evident that the approach of natural church development is by no means theologically neutral. It is unmistakably cross-denominational (neither specifically Baptist, nor Pentecostal, nor Lutheran, etc.), and it can be applied to almost every church tradition. Yet this does not mean that it is neutral in a theological sense. Presenting their thinking as an a-theological methodology has probably been one of the major flaws of the church growth movement.

The bipolar paradigm is characterized by what I like to call the "reformation principle," meaning that all institutions are evaluated on their performance under the following criterion: How useful are they for the development of the dynamic pole, i.e., for the church as an organism? This is at the heart of every reformation movement. It can be demonstrated that the openness of a church or denomination towards the reformation principle—in *practice*, and not in mere mental assent to a "reformation heri-

Outcome of various paradigms

"Bipolar theology"

Danger to the left	Dynamic pole	Static pole	Danger to the right
Dualistic paradigm	**Dynamic pole**	**Static pole**	**Monistic paradigm**
Relativism	Faith	Doctrine	Dogmatism
Eclecticism	Word of God	Biblical Canon	Fundamentalism
Libertinism	Love	Ethics	Legalism
Spiritualism	Fellowship	Sacraments	Sacramentalism
Docetism	Change	Tradition	Traditionalism
Separatism	Multiplication	Cooperation	Monopolism
Individualism	Spiritual gifts	Offices	Clericalism
Anarchism	Social service	Order	Conservatism
Quietism	Evangelism	Proclamation	Universalism

tage"—is directly proportional to its openness to natural church development. The opposite is equally true. It is simply impossible to convince anyone of the merits of this approach as long as he or she is hindered by either spiritualistic or technocratic thinking. For such a person, all spiritual, biblical, or strategic arguments will fail, indeed, must fail.

One should never hope to convince others of the merits of natural church development merely by teaching them the "how-tos." As long as a person's paradigm is not in harmony with this approach, the best "how-to" won't help. It could even be counterproductive to isolate individual "techniques" of natural church development and transplant these into a spiritualistic or technocratic paradigm!

The diagram above illustrates the effects of the three paradigms on various theological issues.

More than methodology

What does this mean practically?

Just what concrete, practical effects does this seemingly abstract concept of "bipolar thinking" have on church development?

In our work at the Institute for Church Development we soon discovered that quantitative evaluation alone is insufficient to depict the growth dynamic of a church. With graph paper and growth curves, we can learn about worship service attendance and other quantitative aspects of church life. What we cannot do, however, is make valid statements about the quality of a church—unless, of course we should equate high worship attendance with high quality.

As we have seen in Part 1, empirical evidence suggests that growth in the areas of the "eight quality characteristics"—i.e., qualitative growth—has a decisive influence on the growth of church worship attendance.

Linear and circular thinking

To illustrate such growth processes, we needed a type of diagram that could integrate both aspects of our bipolar paradigm—quality and quantity, organic and technical thinking. While an arrow represents the linear approach of technical thinking ("From A to B"), the organic view is best illustrated by a circular pattern ("What is the effect of point B on the point of departure A?"). The common mistake made by both technocrats and spiritualists is that they isolate one of the two aspects while disregarding the other (see diagram top right).

In natural church development we try to correlate the two. We have already seen that the New Testament describes the church with examples from both architecture (the technical aspect of building the church) and agriculture (the dynamic and organic aspect of church growth). A combination of the two can be represented as a helix (spiral).

What is a "church helix?"

Our institute has developed a so-called "church helix" in order to facilitate the practical application of this concept. It integrates both the growing and building, organic and technical aspects, both the linear and circular views (see diagram bottom right; cf. pages 43 and 51). The spiral in this diagram represents quantitative growth (development of the church service attendance),

Linear and circular thinking in church development

The "helix" as the synthesis

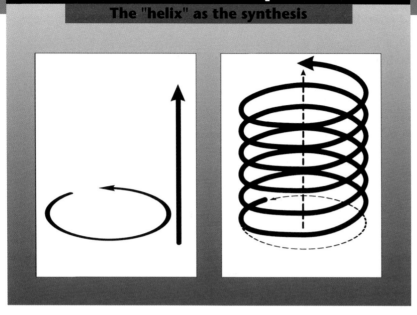

Diagram left: Non-related circular and linear reasoning.
Diagram right: The helix (spiral) as a symbol for the biotic approach—a synthesis of the circular and the linear views.

while the blue areas show the development of individual quality characteristics in a specific church (qualitative growth). While we cannot "produce" higher attendance, we can take concrete action which will increase the quality of church life in the eight quality areas.

This graphic presentation is used to report the results to all churches that request a church analysis. Having used this tool with more than 1000 churches on all six continents, we are confident that there is a demonstrable relationship between the qualitative and quantitative aspects. Attempts to make use of this important insight may, however, be hindered by those whose thinking is shaped by the presuppositions of the spiritualistic or the technocratic approach; they will find it difficult to even begin to understand these complex growth dynamics.

A tool for church analysis

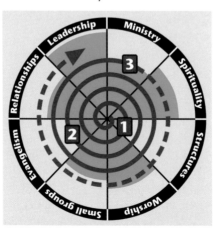

A "church helix" of a typical congregation: The blue sectors represent a church's performance in the eight quality characteristics, while the spiraling arrow shows the development of worship attendance (quantity).

Can we "make" a church grow?

"We cannot 'make' the quantitative growth of churches."

Probably one of the most hotly disputed ecclesial issues today is whether church growth can be "manufactured," that is, attained by human means. The question is, to what extent can we "make" church growth: a little? a lot? not at all? Despite having read many thousands of pages on this issue, I have yet to find a satisfactory answer. It seems to me, however, that we cannot even consider addressing any of the practical issues without a clear answer to this question.

It has been shown that the question is unanswerable when starting with either spiritualistic or technocratic presuppositions. Within the bipolar paradigm, however, the problem is easily solved: the organizational realm of church ministry can be "manufactured"— the organic level can't. One need not even employ extravagant concepts like "paradoxical identity," or "dialectical tension" in order to explain this. It is really quite logical and simple.

The spiritualistic answer

So why all the fuss? Most discussions are monopolized by proponents of either the spiritualistic or the technocratic paradigm (see diagram). A spiritualist, who disassociates the church as an organism from its institutional level, will always claim, "The church (as an organism) cannot be manufactured." Extreme spiritualists can use this as an excuse to lean back in their easy chairs of pious passivity. But what about those spiritualists (and I presume this includes the majority) who sense that this is not the whole truth? They still hold to the belief that church growth cannot be manufactured, yet they are stirred to rather half-hearted attempts to do something after all. What they do and why they do it remains nebulous because of their assumption that nothing can be attained through human effort. At this point, it comes in handy that the spiritualists do not take theological reflection very seriously anyway. More often than not they console themselves with some vague truth about "the mysteries of God."

The technocratic answer

The technocratic paradigm takes a different approach. The church is seen as an organization. Therefore, technocrats should be able to say with confidence, "The church can be manufactured." In the light of biblical evidence, however, no technocrat is truly comfortable with this statement. Even though their

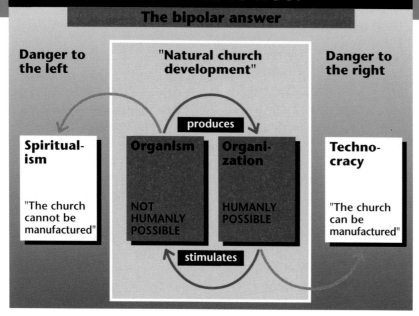

What is humanly possible, and what is not?

The bipolar answer

**Danger to
the left**

**"Natural church
development"**

**Danger to
the right**

produces

**Spiritual-
ism**

"The church
cannot be
manufactured"

Organism

NOT
HUMANLY
POSSIBLE

**Organi-
zation**

HUMANLY
POSSIBLE

**Techno-
cracy**

"The church
can be
manufactured"

stimulates

*The answers of
the three different
paradigms to the
question of
whether we can
"make" a church
grow.*

practical work might reflect a deep conviction of the ability to achieve church growth, their theory seldom reflects this.

Ultimately the two extremes, spiritualist and technocrat, would agree with this statement: "There is really nothing we can do about church development, and yet we ought to do something!" This kind of pseudo-logical paradox is nothing but the result of attempting to harmonize false paradigms with Scripture.

Adopting the bipolar approach removes the need for this type of dialectic. We can refer to the entirely nonparadoxical statement of Paul's, in which he describes the relationship between divine and human involvement: "I planted, Apollos watered, but God gives the increase" (1 Corinthians 3:6). What every farmer knows is obvious in this passage. One plants, waters and harvests. What one cannot do is to cause the growth. Nevertheless, diligence in planting and watering has an influence on the upcoming harvest.

It is not possible to "make" the quantitative growth of churches. Effort and energy should be invested in ensuring that the institutional pole of church life is in harmony with God's principles, so that the organic pole can develop unhindered and healthy. This describes most clearly the strategic approach of natural church development.

**The answer of
natural church
development**

Pragmatism's dead end

"A pragmatist might ask, 'How can I get good fruit without a good tree?'"

The diagram to the right contrasts the three most important differences between natural church development and classical church growth thinking. We have already seen that our approach is not a product of an a-theological philosophy, but is founded upon a reformation principle and paradigm. We have also stated that the goals of natural church development focus on quality rather than quantity. In this section, I want to show a third difference directly related to the two mentioned above: natural church development rejects a merely *pragmatic* mind-set and replaces it with a *principle-oriented* approach.

In order to critically appraise pragmatism in church growth, one must understand why it plays such a significant role in the church growth movement. This becomes evident when we see what the church growth movement tried *to fight against*: a Christian ideology which claimed that no one should ever evaluate the fruit of ministry. Some have used the term "pragmatic" when they really meant "non-ideological." The church growth movement rightly subjected itself to the criterion, "What is the outcome of all of our activities?" The question is biblically sound. It is a question that Jesus Himself taught us to ask.

Six dangers of pragmatism

Nevertheless, it is unfortunate that this concern has been labeled "pragmatism." I would like to list six reasons why I believe the pragmatic approach to be unsuitable for church growth.

Rejection of binding principles

1. Pragmatism as a world view is rooted in the a priori rejection of binding principles. While we should not assume that *Christian* authors who use this term have a negative view of biblical principles, it is fitting to ask why they use this term at all, considering its historical background.

Success as an end in itself

2. The pragmatic approach has the inherent danger of making success the ultimate theological criterion. A secular adage states that "nothing succeeds like success." Translated into Christian jargon, this means that "anything contributing to the numerical growth of churches is good. High worship service attendance is living proof that the church is theologically

100

Philosophy, methods, goals compared

What is the difference?

	Philosophy	Goals	Methods
"Classical church growth thinking"	a-theological	quantitative	pragmatic
"Natural church development"	reformation principle	qualitative	principle-oriented

The difference be-tween natural church develop-ment and "classi-cal church growth" can be clearly seen in the three areas of "philosophy," "goals," and "methods."

on the right path." Unfortunately, some church growth authors have fallen into this trap.

3. Pragmatists always ask the same question: "What is most effec- **Short-term** tive in this situation for church growth?" As mentioned pre- **thinking** viously, this is a legitimate and necessary question, which only ideologists think they never need to ask. Pragmatism's answer to this question is insufficient, however, because of an undue concentration on short-term gain. In church development, as in many other areas of life, short-term gains are often short-lived. In the long run, they often turn out to be counterproductive.

4. Pragmatists have a tendency to determine their own opinion **Blind to God's** on what is important for the kingdom of God. They some- **logic** times overlook the fact that "God's ways are higher than our ways." In contrast, a principle-oriented approach strives to conform to growth principles which are biblically founded and empirically verifiable—ones which we *know* will ultimate-ly bear fruit for God's kingdom, even though at present it might not look like it. The end does not always justify the means. God's principles need no improvement.

"Artificial fruit" 5. Pragmatism conflicts with the biblical principle which states that a good tree bears good fruit (Matthew 7:17). This expressly means that the fruit is good *because* the tree is good. Pragmatists may ask, "How can I get good fruit without a good tree?" They will tend to fall for artificial fruit, which requires an efficiently functioning factory rather than a good and living organism. Once this artificial fruit appears in a church, pragmatists even point to it as "proof" that there must be a good tree to have produced such a harvest.

Opportunism 6. Pragmatic thinking easily becomes fertile soil for opportunism. Going generally with the flow, adjusting to questionable current trends, using manipulative marketing methods, even cooperating with corrupt political systems—all for the well-being of the church, of course—these can be consequences of a strongly developed "pragmatic" thinking.

Pragmatism's motto, "nothing succeeds like success," is rejected by natural church development. It holds the opposite view, that churches are successful because they follow clearly defined, biblical principles.

Part 5

Ten action steps

"Quality characteristics," "minimum factor," "biotic principles," and a "new paradigm" are the four building blocks of natural church development which answer the four basic questions of church growth—what, when, how, and why. The "red thread" running through all four parts was the application of what we have called the "all by itself" principle. In this final section of the book, I would like to present a ten-step plan for introducing the four building blocks into the life of a congregation.

How to develop your own program

*"We should not
fool ourselves
into thinking
that 'preaching'
the right prin-
ciples alone will
be enough to
trigger church
development."*

Up to this point, our comments about programs have been largely critical. I have tried to show that programs are valid only for very specific situations, while principles have universal validity. No matter how often a program may have proven to be success-ful, if it is presented as a cure-all for all situations, the result will be confusion.

This does not, however, reduce the value of programs as such. We would not refrain from exercising our arm muscles, just because there is one possibility of misuse: beating someone up. Nor do we need to refrain from designing a program for church development just because some people cannot keep from using programs in a wrong, i.e., legalistic, technocratic, or magical way.

"Quick-wash-cycle" church growth

Programs with a technocratic bent are expected to take care of church growth by a "quick-wash-cycle." Natural church develop-ment, however, resembles organic life. It is a process that takes time. No single measure, be it a church analysis, a consultation, a prayer night, a seminar, or working through a relevant book, will cause the breakthrough. But when all the aforementioned ele-ments and many others work together in concert, long lasting processes of change can be set in motion .

I would like to show how a church can use the following ten steps to design a customized "program" for its own church develop-ment—not "off-the-rack," but "tailor-made." We have found that someone from the outside with experience in natural church development (a consultant, another pastor, a network, etc.) can be of considerable help in this process.

Different points of departure

The ten steps are intentionally phrased in such a way that they can be applied to every conceivable church situation:

- In one congregation the very term "church growth" encoun-ters resistance.

- Another church passionately desires to grow, but watches sadly as the worship attendance drops.

- A third case is a dynamic, growing church looking for ways to structure future church development.

	Standard program	**No program**	**Individual program**
Works...	... if the church's situation matches the conditions the program presupposes	... if the church leadership intuitively does the right things	... if one can be developed
Doesn't work...	... if the situation in the church is different from the one the program presupposes	... if the intuitively made decisions reflect spiritualistic or technocratic rather than biotic thinking	... if one is not able to individualize universal principles

- A fourth congregation is thinking about planting daughter churches and is looking for principles that are valid for any type of church growth.

- And finally a fifth situation might be a newly planted church that has just passed the initial founding phase and is seeking help for ongoing, healthy church development.

This table shows the (relative) importance of programs for natural church development. They are not a must, but can be of help.

In all of these situations—and many more—the following ten steps can be of help. We should not fool ourselves into thinking that "preaching" the right principles alone will be enough to trigger church development. That would be a misunderstanding of the principle-oriented approach. Principles must always be converted into applied programs. Without this step, all of our discussions about church development are in danger of amounting to no more than pleasant "chit-chat."

In the four preceding parts of this book, we have shown what we ourselves can and should do for church development, and what we cannot do, because it is in God's domain. The following action steps will address only our part—the human domain. This is not because I rate the human contribution as being "more important" than God's—as some critics have already prematurely suggested. The real reason behind it is almost trite: this book is meant to be a guide for people, not for God. He does not need this kind of insight to do His part. That is why I want to limit myself strictly to talking about those things that, according to God's will, we humans can do to advance church development.

God needs no handbook—we do

Step 1:
Build spiritual momentum

"Natural church development is not a strategy to create spiritual momentum. It comes in where this momentum already exists."

How should we view the opinion of Christians who profess that "all we can do for church development is to pray?" We have already seen that this phrase is both theologically and empirically untenable. Many Bible passages illustrate that we can do much more for church development than just pray. These "spiritual" sounding phrases, upon closer examination, turn out to be an expression of the type of thinking that we have called the "spiritualistic paradigm."

We should, however, try to understand what people holding those convictions *really* want to say. They do not mean that we can do absolutely nothing but pray. They mean, "Unless prayer, devotion to Christ, and a personal relationship with Him are at the center of all of our activities, our striving amounts only to unfruitful 'busy-ness.'" And that is absolutely right!

The ultimate goal

Church growth itself should never become the motivation for our activities. Not church development, but worship of God is the goal. Church development is done for the sake of worship.

This function does not take away from the significance of our church growth endeavors, but rather bestows on them the highest honor: they are a tool through which people become followers of Christ, and together glorify their heavenly King.

What "divine principles" mean

I have repeatedly called the principles of church development "divine" principles. This expression deserves an explanation. By "divine," I mean created by God. This does not make the principles God-like. We should never confuse that which God has created with God Himself. This is a real danger, because God's creation is so magnificent that one could get carried away. Our enthusiasm is good and right as long as we do not worship the creation instead of the Creator (Romans 1:25). Rather we should let the beauty of God's marvelous creation (along with the biotic principles we find in it) inspire us to praise "the glory of God" (Psalm 19:2).

This basic theological insight has practical consequences. When people first encounter the biotic principles of church development, they are frequently enthused. Whenever that happens, I'm

The new spiritual experiences we often enjoy at mass events do not automatically lead to church growth—yet they can be powerful motivators.

delighted. But we should never confuse our enthusiasm for *principles* with enthusiasm for the *Lord*. People cannot be kept motivated for church development when their motivation is anything other than devotion to Jesus and His work.

If a church does not have this foundation, the other nine steps we are going to describe will likely have very little effect. To put it bluntly: natural church development is not a strategy to *create* spiritual momentum. It comes in where spiritual momentum already exists and shows practical steps to attract more and more people.

Prerequisites for church development

What can be done if a church lacks spiritual momentum? Even here, it certainly can't hurt to identify the minimum factor, set qualitative goals, apply biotic principles, and so forth. But these are not the first and most important steps. The believers first must be gripped by a new devotion to Jesus.

What a church can do

How can we bring this about? There are as many answers to this question as there are Christians on the globe. For some, contact with a "model church" sparked a fire, others were inspired through a large Christian gathering or at a quiet retreat. In and of themselves, these kinds of events will never set church growth in motion—as some erroneously believe and teach. They can, however, get people to start asking the question, "How can the things I experienced here become part of the everyday life of our congregation?"

Step 2: Determine your minimum factors

"When we try to identify our church's minimum factor by intuition alone, we are often way off the mark."

Most groups embark on natural church development by determining their "minimum factors"—those least developed quality characteristics which at present seriously hinder development.

There is no church without a "minimum factor." The term does not necessarily mean that a church is "bad" in a certain area—we have even identified churches whose minimum factor area is a model for other churches! It simply means that the seven other areas are better developed than the minimum factor. It also means that concentrating on that low point will bring lasting progress in that congregation's development.

Why intuition often fails

Over the past years, I have noticed that when people try to identify their church's minimum factors by intuition alone, they are often way off the mark. In fact, it is not unusual for them to think that the area of their greatest strength is their minimum factor!

How can this happen? Usually these churches have extremely high quality standards in this area. They also have a very developed awareness of all potential problems, and, therefore, a keen eye for possible improvements. Other areas of church life that are not as important to them, however, they hardly seem to notice. To reliably identify a church's minimum factors—instead of going on assumptions—I recommend that every church obtain a church profile based on a scientifically sound analysis.

How a church profile is obtained

One of the goals of our research was the development of a testing procedure through which every interested church could easily identify its minimum factors. For this analysis, about 30 church members (and the pastor) complete a questionnaire. The items do not ask members to *appraise* the church ("On a scale from one to ten, how loving is your church?"), but to describe *actual behavior* (e.g., "How often have you invited someone from the church over for a meal or a cup of coffee in the past two months?").

Our analysis compares the data from these responses with the roughly 4 million previously collected answers and creates a "church profile." The results are displayed in a chart that shows

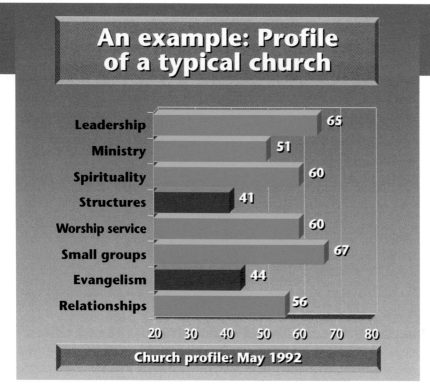

An example: Profile of a typical church

Leadership 65
Ministry 51
Spirituality 60
Structures 41
Worship service 60
Small groups 67
Evangelism 44
Relationships 56

20 30 40 50 60 70 80

Church profile: May 1992

A typical church profile: The quality characteristics "functional struc-tures" and "need-oriented evange-lism" were the least developed at the time of the survey.

the strengths and weaknesses of a church at first glance (see chart above).

The questionnaires can be processed by a Natural Church Develop-ment consultant or by the church itself. In the latter case, you must attend a Natural Church Development Basic Training event to ob-tain the CORE software. The program is continually updated and is based on the norms of all previously researched congregations. Any new insights resulting from ongoing research in other churches are automatically included in the computer evaluation process.

The advantage of a scientific process

When a church profile is obtained this way, the church can be sure that the resulting values are exactly normed and comparable with others. The formula used for this process is reliable, because it is based on the data of the more than 1000 researched churches. In the first few years of our ministry, when we used far less sophisti-cated methods to produce church profiles, I learned that although some insights can be gained with much less effort, they cannot serve as the basis for a truly reliable planning process. If you are interested in having a church profile for your congregation, please refer to the information on page 128.

Step 3:
Set qualitative goals

"What would happen if the quality of each of the eight areas would double?"

What is a "qualitative goal?" To put it plainly, "qualitative" has nothing "fuzzy" about it! Qualitative goals are precise, time-bound, verifiable, measurable goals which relate to the *increase of quality in a church.*

It is not a "qualitative goal" when a church member says, "I want to become a better Christian," or when a church declares, "In the future we want relate to each other in a more loving and spiritual way." These are nice statements, but they are not goals. The box on the right has some examples of what I mean by qualitative goals.

Continual quality increase

When we set goals, we need to do so in areas we can actually influence. This is the main reason why goals aimed at increased worship attendance figures are often counterproductive (see pages 44-45). In contrast, the quality of the eight key areas of church life can definitely be affected by our work. What else, indeed, should be the goal of church planning, if not the continual increase of its quality? Should we leave it to chance whether Christians learn to discern their gifts, or to relate to each other in loving ways, whether they have a time and place for spiritual sharing, or find their part in fulfilling the Great Commission?

What can I contribute?

In my seminars, after the eight quality characteristics have been discussed, I often ask, "What would happen if the quality of each of the eight areas would double within the next twelve months?" Almost anybody who thinks about this question—even if he or she does not know the principles of natural church development in all detail—will realize that this would set off an enormous transformation process which would deserve our full and passionate involvement.

Then I ask, "What can we do in each of the eight areas in order to produce this quality increase?" This question leads us right into the goal-setting process. The problem in many churches is that the leadership talks about all kinds of questions, but never tackles those concrete things the church should do, plan for, pray about, and support to keep increasing the quality of church life in the eight areas mentioned above.

Area of ministry	Examples of qualitative goals
Leadership	"By the end of the year, our pastor will be released from 20 percent of his regular responsibilities in order to dedicate this time to the training of lay workers"
Ministry	"At the end of nine months 80 percent of those attending worship services will have discovered their spiritual gifts and 50 percent will be active in a ministry corresponding to their gifts"
Spirituality	"By February 1 we will have decided which of the three lay workers under consideration will assume coordination of the prayer ministry"
Structures	"By the end of December this year, we will have determined a point person for each of the nine areas of ministry our church has established"
Worship service	"From the beginning of next year, we will have a worship service each quarter which is specifically designed to reach non-Christians"
Small groups	"Within the next six months, we will divide our home Bible study with the co-leader assuming the leadership of the new group"
Evangelism	"By the end of April the church leadership will have identified which 10 percent of the Christians God has blessed with the gift of evangelism and will have had a personal conversation with each one regarding this gift"
Relationships	"After having studied the 'Learning to Love Process' for three months, each home Bible study participant will agree with the statement: 'I am enjoying being a part of this fellowship more than in the past.'"

In this chart, you will find one example of a "qualitative goal" for each of the eight quality characteristics. Please note that the examples are randomly chosen illustrations. There are no standard goals for all churches—each church must set goals that promise the greatest possible progress in church development under their given circumstances.

111

Step 4:
Identify obstacles

"Not everything
that is spiritu-
ally desirable
can actually be
carried off in a
church."

All of the qualitative goals described in the last chapter can be reached by taking practical steps, provided this is what the church members really *want*. This, however, is the core problem. Many churches fail to reach their goals—and then interpret their defeat as proof that quality increase isn't "humanly possible" after all. I think this interpretation is mistaken. The problem is not that the measures needed to reach the goal just "can't be done," but rather that some Christians just *don't want* what "can be done" to actually happen.

Identifying these hindrances brings us to the down-to-earth realities which have existed since Jesus walked on earth and will not leave us until His return. Church development always involves real people carrying with them their past experiences, hurts, fears, and defense mechanisms. Not everything that is spiritually desirable can actually be carried off in a church. If we tried to ignore reality, our deliberations would be nothing but pipe dreams.

Recognizing resistance

At a pastors' conference where I was speaking on natural church development, I explained our offer to determine the minimum factor for churches. One pastor immediately objected, "You don't mean to suggest that each church ought to have such a survey, do you? There are many reasons against it!"

I thanked him for his comment and laid a blank transparency on the overhead projector. On it I wrote "Reasons against doing a survey," and asked the pastor to name his three most important reasons. Then I sat down—and waited. For two oppressively long minutes, an icy silence filled the room. I finally broke the silence by saying, "This transparency has a complete listing of all the reasons there are against obtaining a church profile."

Why rational arguments often can't help

Today I am ashamed of my behavior. However, I still firmly believe that the point I was making was right. There is no real reason *not* to have a church profile done. In the very worst possible scenario, the church leadership would disagree with the profile and throw it away. All they would lose would be a little bit of money—and they wouldn't risk even that, because in such a case we would gladly return the fees!

112

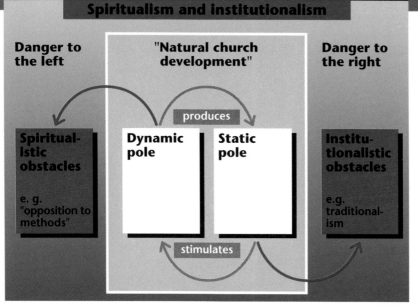

Obstacles due to false paradigms

Spiritualism and institutionalism

Danger to the left

"Natural church development"

Danger to the right

produces

Spiritual-istic obstacles

e. g. "opposition to methods"

Dynamic pole

Static pole

Institu-tionalistic obstacles

e.g. traditional-ism

stimulates

Most hindrances to natural church development can be traced to the two false paradigms. Neither side relates naturally to church structures.

Yes, rationally my arguments were right. What I didn't see was that this pastor's problem was not a rational problem at all. When I spoke with him in person after the meeting, I sensed that he was controlled by fear that such a survey could "expose" him and his ministry. My. rational arguments had not helped at all; they had made the situation even worse!

Whenever we encounter resistance to natural church develop-ment, we should be sensitive to the reasons hidden behind the "rational" objections. In the final analysis, most obstacles are rooted in the false paradigms mentioned in this book.

Find out the real reasons

Considering that entire faith and value systems are affected by theological paradigms, it is not surprising that the discussions are often so emotional. For a traditionalist or a spiritualist, the questions we raise are much more than deliberations about strategy. The "essence of faith," as they understand it, is at stake.

Step 5:
Apply biotic principles

"The biotic principles should be seen as a checklist that can be applied to every decision we face."

Once we encounter resistance from within our churches or from without—if not sooner—we will realize just how helpful the principle-oriented approach is in everyday church life. In Part 3 we mentioned that biotic principles are very useful for helping us to *react* constructively in the midst of situations which we have not chosen ourselves.

One weakness of much of church growth literature has been its focus on being a guide to proper *action*, whereas any form of *reaction* has been viewed with suspicion. It is doubtless correct that no one can lead by "reaction" alone.

On the other hand, it is a proven fact that leaders—be they "proactive" or "reactive"—spend the greatest portion of their time responding to challenges that arise in their environment. It is in the midst of these everyday decisions, and nowhere else, that one realizes whether the biotic approach has truly been internalized—or if it has remained just an abstract theory.

A tool for everyday decisions

The "six biotic principles" should be seen as a "checklist" that can be applied to every decision faced. The following page has an actual example: a new full-time worker is to be hired. How should he or she be financed?

The middle column (Solution 1) shows a reaction without reference to biotic principles. The column on the right (Solution 2) presents the conscious use of biotic principles in the decision-making process. Obviously this is very abbreviated and simplified. Nevertheless, it shows the differences between a biotic and a purely pragmatic strategy for problem-solving. This pattern can be used for most decision making in church life.

Having used such checklists extensively in my seminars, I have learned that non-theologians generally have much less difficulty with this way of thinking than theologians. Standard theological education apparently trains us in "reductionist" rather than "integrated" thinking. Most of us should probably practice this way of thinking on paper for a while before we try it in real life.

The problem	Solution 1 (technocratic)	Solution 2 (biotic)
A new full-time worker is to be hired to lead the small group ministry.	The church finances will be adjusted so that the salary for the new position is available. Budget cuts in other areas are unavoidable.	Only 20 percent of the salary will come from the church budget, the rest through contributions from those who benefit from the new position. In the beginning, it will be a half-time position, which—once the ministry and finances have expanded—can be made into a full-time position.
Interdependence	A weakness of this solution is that the problem of financing is viewed in isolation from the total dynamic of a healthy church organism. This leads to shortsighted conclusions: "We lack the money, so we must save elsewhere."	This solution takes into account the relationship of finances to other areas of church life, such as the effects on the motivation and thought structure of church members, on personal giving, on how the new staff person views oneself, etc.
Multiplication	This kind of thinking all but rules out a continual multiplication of the ministry (at least for paid personnel). The financial resources are preprogrammed to gradually diminish until they are entirely depleted.	Since the new staff person is practically "self-financed," almost unlimited multiplication is possible. There is no reason why, according to this model, another, or a third or fourth staff person cannot be added, if the need arises.
Energy transformation	It is overlooked that it is almost always less attractive to donate to an institution than to an individual.	The assumption here is that once people get a taste of what is possible (i.e., they observe the impact of their financial gift), they will be more open to giving to this project again.
Multi-usage	This solution hardly has a positive effect on other areas. On the contrary, it is more likely that the tightened finances will make the congregation skeptical about the new position and thus may negatively influence the entire home Bible study ministry.	The word of the new staff person contributes to his or her own finances. This steers both the staff member and the donor in a growth-oriented direction right from the start.
Symbiosis	A weakness of this solution is that one is fixed on a single means of financing (monoculture), rather than making use of the symbiotic effect of various systems.	The solution combines various systems (church budget plus donations plus future possibilities for expansion). These cross-pollinate and have a synergistic effect.
Functionality	It follows from what was stated above that this solution, though it makes the new position possible in the short run, does not promote growth in the long run. This type of thinking will inevitably cause church growth to stagnate once a certain size is reached.	This harmonizes with the principle that every organic system must develop self-supportive sub-systems once it reaches a certain size if it is to continue to grow. It is definitely possible to test the "fruit" of this approach!

Step 6:
Exercise your strengths

We have already noted the caricature of the minimum strategy says that we should always concentrate on what we do least well. Natural church development has a different approach. Its motto is: "Find your strengths, develop them, enjoy them, use them. What for? In order to make progress in the area of your minimum factor."

Now what are the strengths of your church? In thinking through this question, you should frame it in the following four ways:

1. Your strongest quality characteristics (**"maximum factors"**). No matter what they may be, whether "leadership" or "evangelism" or something else, you should ask this question: How can these strengths be used more effectively to work on our points of weakness? This question has proven to be very creative, because it starts with what God has obviously used in the past and what the church is already comfortable with. While it sometimes stirs up fears to isolate a church's minimum factor, beginning with the strengths sets a positive tone.

2. Your **"spiritual culture."** Every church has developed its own style of living out faith in Jesus Christ. There is nothing wrong with that, as long we are really dealing with spiritual cultures, and not with theologically disguised unbelief. The unique way in which a church expresses its devotion to Christ should always be valued as a strength. It is because of our differences in expressing our spirituality that we can expect to appeal to people who could never be reached by the "spiritual culture" of other churches.

3. **Contextual factors.** Each church has some characteristics that are "givens," not because of choice but because of contextual factors, such as the location (city or rural), the social status of the population, or the facilities available for ministry. No other church in the whole wide world has exactly the same context as yours!

4. **Spiritual Gifts.** The greatest strength of each church is the treasure of spiritual gifts that God has already given to the members. I am *not* referring to the quality characteristic "gift-

Strengths	Minimum factors
for example:	for example:
• Maximum factors	• Ministry
• Spiritual culture	• Structures
• Contextual factors	• Small groups
• Spiritual gifts	• Relationships

The motto of natural church development: Use strengths to work on the church's minimum factors.

oriented ministry." Even if this quality characteristic is hardly developed in your church, you can be sure that all the gifts God has given for the fulfillment of the Great Commission are already present among His people. They just need to be discovered. Anybody skeptical about the relevance of the concept of "biotic potential" for the church should study the biblical teaching on spiritual gifts. We can't "make" gifts, but we can certainly release what God has already invested in Christians. The closer we get to God's design, the more we will experience the "self-organization" of many areas in church life.

Results in all areas

No matter what quality characteristic we are working on, the concept of spiritual gifts is basic. What should "empowering leaders" do but help Christians release the potential that God has invested in them? How can "gift-oriented ministry" work if Christians aren't even aware of their spiritual gifts? How can "passionate spirituality" flow when many are frustrated by always serving God where they don't fit? What are "functional structures" if not the means to match God-given gifts with the corresponding tasks? How can a worship service be more "inspiring" than when Christians freely participate with all kinds of gifts? What makes small groups "holistic" but Christians serving one another with the gifts that God has given them? How can "need-oriented evangelism" take place if the church doesn't even know who among them has the gift of evangelism? Finally, can we honestly talk about "loving relationships" if we fail to help church members find the place that God has prepared for them in the Body of Christ? All the alternatives I have found so far to the gift-oriented approach were not exactly distinguished by loving attitudes.

Step 7:
Utilize NCD tools

"Can you imagine what might happen if 60% of those regularly attending worship would go through a twelve-month course focused on growing in love?"

All deliberations about natural church development will remain static as long as the majority of church members are not integrated into the growth process. This is why our Institute has developed work materials to help with the practical implementation of each of the eight quality characteristics (see right). In the English language these NCD tools will be translated and published in the series "NCD Discipleship Resources." What distinguishes these "biotic materials" from others?

1. The NCD Discipleship Resources are designed to apply the **biotic principles** without using the corresponding technical terms. None of the workbooks makes reference to "growth automatisms," "energy transformation," or the "minimum strategy." These theoretical concepts are not addressed in the workbooks, but they are the foundational strategical background.

2. While most other church growth materials specifically address church leadership, the NCD Discipleship Resources are aimed at **individual church members**. They are designed to be used by individual Christians, small groups, and whole churches, with the emphasis being on the small group audience. Every workbook has a corresponding leader's handbook that shows how the material can be presented in units of one, three, six, or twelve lessons.

3. While the purpose of this book is to explain principles, the NCD Discipleship Resources go one step further: they help with the **programmed application** of the principles. They are "reproducible systems" that can be used by lay-people without the help of church leadership. In contrast to other "programs" (which sometimes treat every Christian alike), the biotic materials encourage individuality, spontaneity, and creativity.

4. As we developed these materials, we tried to **learn from other programs and approaches**. We searched through materials (mostly "model-oriented") from all over the world, looking for universally applicable principles. We now have internationally conceptualized masters for the eight quality characteristics, available in contextualized editions for different countries.

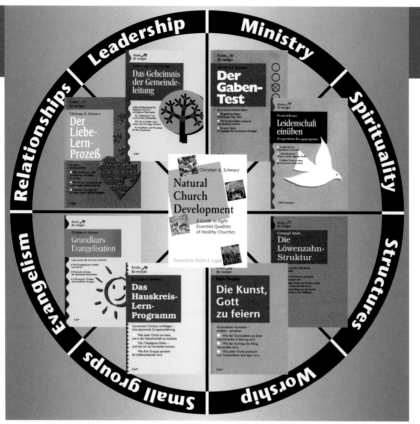

For each of the eight quality characteristics we offer workbooks in different languages. They are all based on the biotic principles described in this book. Pictured here are the materials of the German edition.

Can you imagine, for instance, what might happen if 60 percent of those regularly attending worship would go through a twelve-month small group course focused on growing in love? People would probably end up crying some tears, laughing a lot, becoming reconciled, getting conflicts out in the open, and gaining a new understanding of God's love. The term "church growth" would probably not even be mentioned. And yet, such a learning process demonstrably has a tremendous impact on the growth of a church—certainly greater than if the leadership just talks or the pastor just preaches about love.

Practical application instead of mere talk

This example relates to what I have learned in recent years about how the "law of critical mass" works in churches. As long as only a minority in the church really supports church development, it will be a very tedious and frustrating task. But once a clear majority has become active in the growth process, another element of "spiritual self-organization" comes into play. Many things that leaders have dreamed about suddenly begin to happen "all by themselves."

The "law of critical mass"

Step 8:
Monitor effectiveness

"As a rule of thumb, we recommend a profile update twice a year."

Once the minimum factor of a church has been identified and measures taken to improve in this area, how can we make sure that real fruit has developed? One of the easiest and most precise methods is to have another church profile done (see pages 108-109).

The results, particularly the comparison of the two profiles, clearly show the development of the quality indices in each of the eight areas. Should a church find out that nothing has changed in the minimum area, it would be advisable to keep concentrating on this "sore spot." Should it be found that the interventions have borne fruit (which is the case in about 90 percent of the churches we analyzed more than once), then the focus should be on the new minimum factors.

Comparing two profiles

Each church profile, as we have already seen, is like a snapshot. Some church leaders, who have had their church profiled only once, have confused the results with the "essential character of their church." I want to seriously warn against such a static view of the church profile. The fact is that the values in all eight areas change fairly quickly, especially if the church is consciously working on them.

The two boxes show how church profiles can be compared. This example is of a church that is typical of those we have researched. The box to the left shows the results of an older survey (blue bars), compared to a new one (yellow bars). You will notice that the church made by far the greatest progress (+14) in the area of its minimum factor ("functional structures"). Their work has clearly paid off!

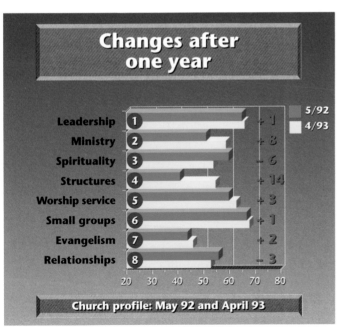

Changes after one year

| | | | 5/92 |
| | | | 4/93 |

Leadership	1	+ 1
Ministry	2	+ 8
Spirituality	3	− 6
Structures	4	+ 14
Worship service	5	+ 3
Small groups	6	+ 1
Evangelism	7	+ 2
Relationships	8	− 3

20 30 40 50 60 70 80

Church profile: May 92 and April 93

Of more interest than an analysis of the absolute figures is a **Look for** closer look at the changes in the values of the eight quality **developments** characteristics (box right). We can clearly see progress in most **and trends** areas, such as in "structures" (4) and "ministry" (2)—but two areas have decreased: "spirituality" (3) and "relationships" (8). These indicate potential future problems. A graphic presentation like this allows the church to follow the development trends (positive or negative) in each of the eight areas. It is very helpful to monitor these developments for responsible church growth planning.

At what intervals should church profiles be made? The answer **The time** depends on how intensively a church is working on improving **interval** its minimum factors. Some churches we researched showed **between** measurable differences after only a few weeks, but normally it **profiles** takes several months for a significant quality increase to develop. As a rule of thumb, we recommend a profile update twice a year, in order to be able to compare the results. Six months is usually enough time to make significant progress in the minimum factor area, even in complex church situations. On the other hand, six months is not so long that the necessary changes are in danger of being postponed until the thirtieth of February—next year!

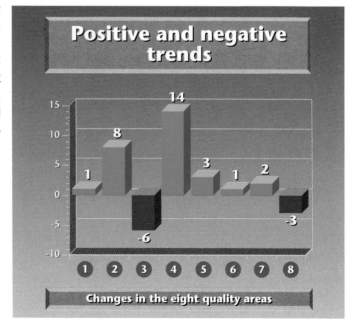

Positive and negative trends

Changes in the eight quality areas

Step 9: Address your new minimum factors

Work on a church's "minimum factors" is a continual process, not a one-time event. At least one of the eight quality characteristics always deserves special attention from the church leadership, and one can confidently expect that energy invested in that area will benefit the overall development of the congregation.

The chart on the right graphically shows the development of the "sample church" we discussed in the previous chapter over a period of three years. Notice that although the eight areas do not show a steady increase, but rather up-and-down movements, the overall tendency is upward.

Focusing attention on one of the eight quality characteristics does not always immediately produce quantitative growth. Sometimes a church must painstakingly work on two or three minimum factors before quantitative fruit shows.

This example shows how important it is to monitor the development of qualitative growth in a church over a longer period of time. As long as the development is generally positive, quantitative growth can sooner or later be expected.

The direction is important

Neither the absolute *level* of quality reached, nor the *speed* with which improvements are made is decisive—although both are worth striving for. The most important factor is the *direction* in which the quality index is moving. Does it tend upwards or downwards? Any quality increase—even if it seems negligible and even if the church has not yet experienced numerical growth—is real progress in the church development process. A fixation on quantitative increase as the true sign of success seems to me a very static way of thinking.

Conversely, should the development of the quality index take a negative turn, a church must realistically anticipate serious problems—even if at the moment it is growing dynamically. Unless corrective measures are taken—and often they are not because things are going so well—this church might soon join the ranks of stagnating or decreasing congregations.

With the quality index measure as a tool, consistent monitoring of church quality has been made possible. It is a much more helpful and descriptive instrument for "success control" in

Development of the quality index

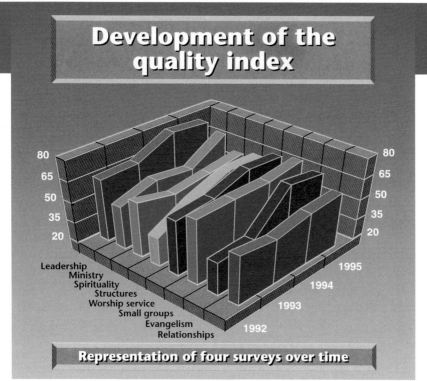

80
65
50
35
20

80
65
50
35
20

Leadership
Ministry
Spirituality
Structures
Worship service
Small groups
Evangelism
Relationships

1995
1994
1993
1992

Representation of four surveys over time

The chart shows the further qualitative development of our sample church. Behind each up or down movement there are stories of prayers, decisions, crises, and successes.

church development than any growth charts or statistics of worship attendance.

Our international research data allow any church to do its own profile surveys via computer. This makes it possible for regular quality control to become a fixed "institution." Any time the church needs reliable data, it can easily do the survey, process the data, and present the results much like in the graph above. This provides a dependable basis for planning further steps.

I sincerely hope that in the future surveys like these will no longer cause fear and trembling—as is still the case in many places—but might become a normal "behind the scenes" support activity of the church. Church quality control should become as routine as keeping track of worship attendance or giving.

Continual quality control

Step 10:
Multiply your church

In the course of our reflections, we have seen over and again that growth is not unlimited in God's creation. A healthy organism doesn't keep growing indefinitely, but brings forth other organisms, which in their turn also multiply. The same biotic principle that can be applied to life within a church (e.g., multiplication of groups, workers, or resources) is also valid for the church as a whole. If the church is healthy, it will eventually reproduce.

Some Christians who carry the banner of church planting would go so far as to count the "reproduction of new churches" as an additional quality characteristic of a healthy church. This is certainly one way to look at it. I would propose, however, that it is methodically more consistent not to add the question of reproduction as a ninth element to our church helix. It should be *a different perspective* from which to view the helix, using two questions: "How did this organism, which is defined by the eight quality characteristics, get started?", and "How can such an organism come into being again today?"

How a church comes into being

With the exception of technocratically installed artificial constructs, every church has at some point been "planted" (see diagram right). Church consultant Robert Logan identifies four phases in the origin of a church: reproduction, conception, prenatal, and birth. During each of these four phases the important task is to nurture the development of the eight quality characteristics in an appropriate way.

Let's have a closer look at one of the four phases, the prenatal phase. The reproduction and conception phases have designed the new church, that is, they have developed a master plan for the practical realization of all eight areas. In the prenatal phase, these quality characteristics are practiced within the church planting team. Normally the development follows this pattern: it begins with a team of leaders (quality characteristic 1) who recruit qualified co-workers (quality characteristic 2). Right from the start they try to live out passionate spirituality (quality characteristic 3) and to build deep relationships among the founding members (quality characteristic 8). This happens primarily in the context of a small group (quality characteristic 6). Even in this initial phase,

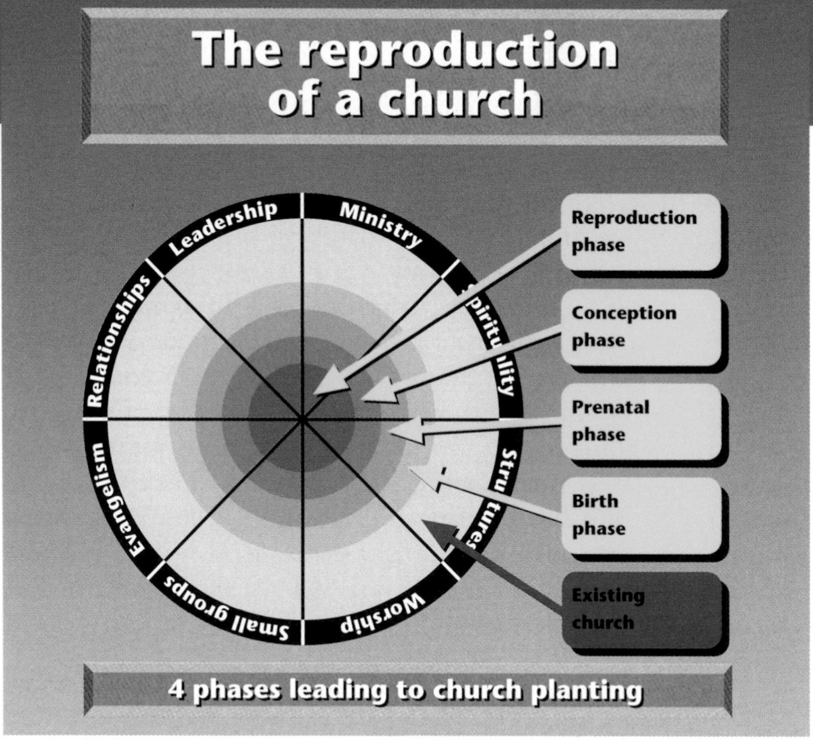

The reproduction of a church

4 phases leading to church planting

Labels in diagram: Leadership, Ministry, Relationships, Spirituality, Structures, Evangelism, Small groups, Worship

Reproduction phase

Conception phase

Prenatal phase

Birth phase

Existing church

This diagram shows the four phases in the development of a new church (yellow boxes) which must occur before we can call it an "existing church" (red box). In each of these four phases it is important to help all eight quality characteristics to take hold.

these Christians are keyed not to hide their faith but to find their personal modes of evangelism (quality characteristic 7). The embryonic structures of the new church begin to emerge (quality characteristic 4). And finally, the transition from the prenatal to the birth phase is signaled by the very first corporate worship services (quality characteristic 5).

A law of life

The moment a church celebrates its first *public* worship service, we say that a new church has been born. From then on, it is no longer a "church-planting project," but an "existing church" that needs to carefully guard its health, learn to conquer diseases, and grow quantitatively and qualitatively. It is extremely helpful for such a new church—right from the beginning—to build spiritual momentum, determine its minimum factors, set qualitative goals, identify obstacles, apply biotic principles, exercise its strengths, use biotic materials, etc.

And what if this church exists for a while, and with God's help grows qualitatively and quantitatively? Then the whole process will be repeated—another church will be born. This is how life is reproduced everywhere in God's creation. Surprisingly, the church of Jesus Christ has often overlooked these very basic laws of life.

Church growth in the power of the Holy Spirit

"Church growth in the power of the Holy Spirit does not mean ignoring God's principles."

Some Christians think that the principles covered in this book are "not really spiritual." They don't exactly fight them, and they might even use one of them from time to time, but, to put it mildly, they don't get excited about them either. For them, the work of the Holy Spirit is something entirely different than the principles described in this book.

I have sought to show that such a view, as widespread as it may be, has more affinity to a spiritualistic paradigm than to the Holy Spirit we encounter in the Bible. Church growth in the power of the Holy Spirit does not mean ignoring God's principles. It means putting those principles to work in our churches as much as possible, even when they seem unusual, hard to follow, go against our tradition, or even hurt.

All-powerful human beings?

Natural church development is a declared enemy of any attempts to build the church of Jesus Christ in one's own strength. By this I don't mean an attack on imaginary self-confident Christians who proclaim, "Why do we need the Holy Spirit? Our own methods work by themselves!" I have never once encountered such audacity. No, what I mean by church growth "in one's own strength," is something altogether different. I think of Christians who very consciously want to work in the power of the Holy Spirit, but who for all practical purposes substitute human efforts for the work of God.

Anytime we disregard the fundamental church growth principles that we learn from Scripture and which are validated by our experience; anytime we ignore the growth automatisms with which God Himself builds His church; and anytime we try—whether through ignorance or through spiritual arrogance—to use ineffective and resource-devouring methods, *that* is when we are acting in our own strength.

Natural church development is made up of principles God has created and revealed to us. This theme is woven through this whole book.

It does not mean, however, that a book like this claims "divine authorship." That would be absurd. No, the *terminology* we have chosen to describe these principles is less than perfect. The *research techniques* we used to empirically identify the principles are flawed—like any scientific method. And the *materials* we have developed can be improved. But all of this does not change one basic fact: the *principles* that we have gropingly tried to search out and blunderingly tried to communicate find their source in God.

Unfortunately we have been able to touch on many topics in this book only briefly. This publication is an attempt to produce a simplified first introduction to natural church development based on what I have covered more extensively in several other books.

Set the sails!

Remember the illustration from the introduction. In a symbolic way, it depicts our attempts to set the church in motion in our own strength (see left). In the terms of a new picture (see below), what would church development in the power of the Holy Spirit mean?

First of all, it would mean an end to the "push and shove" in church life. Second, it would mean that we would finally use the wonderfully round "wheels" that are already heaped up in the cart, instead of insisting that using the square ones is more honoring to God! And third, it would mean that we would set the sails that are buried under the wheels, and pray that God might send us the powerful wind of His Holy Spirit.

Then we might even climb into the cart ourselves and discover that God likes nothing better than to answer those prayers.

The next steps

For further information and help in applying the principles of *Natural Church Development* in the life of your congregation or denomination, please use the contact information below to learn more about the following resources:

Implementation Guide to "Natural Church Development"
Christian Schwarz and Christoph Schalk
This book goes inside the concepts raised in *Natural Church Development*. It answers a host of frequently raised questions and provides practical, step-by-step guidance to help you discover and develop the God-given, unique nature of your congregation. (214 pages)

ABC's of Natural Church Development
Christian Schwarz
This booklet summarizes the key concepts of *Natural Church Development* in an informative and easy-reading style. This provides an ideal way to introduce the concept to your staff, board, or congregation. (32 pages)

Congregational Survey Kit for "Natural Church Development"
Christian Schwarz and Christoph Schalk
This widely tested kit provides one survey for the pastoral staff and 30 copies of a second survey designed for actively involved laypeople in the church. The package includes a tally and report after you submit the completed surveys. The idea is to identify your congregation's "minimum factor" and then develop an action plan for strengthening it.

Releasing Your Church's Potential
Robert E. Logan and Thomas T. Clegg with Jeanette Buller
This new resource guides you through the process of designing and implementing change in your personal life, ministry, and church. Anchored to the eight essential qualities of *Natural Church Development*, the kit contains cassette tapes, prayer guides, outlines, reflection questions, action checklists, and worksheets designed to increase your church's health. (10 audiocassettes plus a 266-page notebook in 10 chapter segments)

The Leadership Centre
P.O. Box 41083 RPO South
Winfield, BC Canada V4V 1Z7
Phone: 800-804-0777 (North America)
Phone: 250-766-0907
Fax: 250-766-0912
Email: office@GrowingLeadership.com
Website: www.GrowingLeadership.com